Some people s

GOD IS NO LAUGHING MATTER

Some people say . . .

GOD IS NO LAUGHING MATTER

*An Artist's Observations and
Objections on the Spiritual Path*

JULIA CAMERON

JEREMY P. TARCHER/PUTNAM
a member of Penguin Putnam Inc.
NEW YORK

Most Tarcher/Putnam books are available at special quantity discounts for bulk purchase for sales promotions, premiums, fund-raising, and educational needs. Special books or book excerpts also can be created to fit specific needs. For details, write Putnam Special Markets, 375 Hudson Street, New York, NY 10014.

Jeremy P. Tarcher/Putnam
a member of
Penguin Putnam Inc.
375 Hudson Street
New York, NY 10014
www.penguinputnam.com

First Trade Paperback Edition 2001

The Library of Congress cataloged the hardcover edition as follows:
Cameron, Julia.
God is no laughing matter : an artist's observations and objections on the spiritual path/Julia Cameron.
p.   cm.
ISBN 1-58542-065-4
1. Spiritual life.   I. Title.
BL624.C3319   2000   00-044710
291.4'4—dc21

ISBN 1-58542-128-6 (paperback edition)

Printed in the United States of America
1   3   5   7   9   10   8   6   4   2

This book is printed on acid-free paper. ♾

*Book design by Jennifer Daddio
and Claire Vaccaro*

*I would like to take "One Step Beyond" and
dedicate this book to director John Newland
in his new land.*

ACKNOWLEDGMENTS

Elizabeth Cameron

Sara Carder

Heidi Castleman

Sonia Choquette

Dan Conroy

Joel Fotinos

Natalie Goldberg

Michael Graham

Rosemarie Greco

Sister Julia Clare Greene, B.V.M.

Christina Grof

David Groff

Gerard Hackett

Bernice Hill

Elberta Honstein

Jo Ann Ianotti

Arnold Jones

Bill LaVallee

Emma Lively

Larry Lonergan

Julianna McCarthy

James Navé

John Newland

Domenica Cameron Scorsese

Max Showalter

Jeremy Tarcher

Ed Towle

Claire Vaccaro

Rosemary Welden

CONTENTS

Some people say . . .

GOD IS NO LAUGHING MATTER

INTRODUCTION

When I published *The Artist's Way* in 1992, I had been a working writer for more than two decades, writing novels, plays, movies, short stories, television, poetry, and songs. My identity was that of a working artist. Over the years, I had devised a set of tools to keep myself unblocked. Those tools— a working set of artist's spiritual tools—were personal and pragmatic, and born out of my own creative experience.

Although we seldom view it this way, creativity is a spiritual path and yields many spiritual insights. Nothing teaches more patience than the third draft of a long novel. Nothing teaches more humility and acceptance than a stingingly cruel review. Few things teach more spiritual wonder than the sudden flash of creative inspiration—a vision, really, that calls you into the service of a piece of art, service that lasts years or even decades as you work to bring the vision to life.

Making art is truly a vocation. (From the Latin *vocare*, "to call.") Artists are *called* to make art. It was, and is, the making of art that teaches me my spiritual lessons.

When *The Artist's Way* sold upward of a million copies, I found myself suddenly known not for my primary work but for its by-product—the tools I had devised to keep myself and my artist friends unblocked. In the public eye and in the press, I was positioned and perceived as a "creativity expert" and a "spiritual teacher." Arguably, I *am* both of those things, but they are a distillate of my primary identity as an artist. It is the making of art that fills my days, morning to night. It is the making of art that teaches me my spiritual tools—a central fact that can easily get misplaced and often did, if not by me then by others.

Abruptly catapulted into what I call the "spirituality circuit," I was invited to share Web sites and teaching venues with everyone from Deepak Chopra to the Dalai Lama. I was asked to conduct creativity lectures on cruises and in power spots around the globe. Spirituality, it seemed, was big business, and so, it seemed, was I. Instead of a person, I was suddenly a product, even a name brand. (You can imagine how this felt—was there really a "spiritual need" for *The Artist's Way for Dentists*?) I was approached to endorse beauty books *(The Artist's Way for Models?)*. Sometimes it seemed everyone had an idea of who I should be on their terms, and none of who I was on my own.

I was asked to do anything and everything except be

what I really was—a floor sample of my own tool kit, sharing artist to artist. I had a daily battle to keep time and space to answer my own creative callings: the poetry, music, novels, and plays that wanted to be written no matter what. Cast as a generic spiritual teacher, I often felt as if I were an actor in a play where I'd been wildly miscast.

As an artist with an artist's eye, I often found myself viewing the current spiritual terrain a little differently than a lot of people. I saw comedy where others were seeing high drama. I saw farce where others presented morality plays. Like Dorothy peeping behind the curtain at the Wizard of Oz, I often saw the familiar machinations of show business and commerce as the hidden engine behind the solemn and holy front being presented to a spiritually hungry public.

As a writer-director with years in Hollywood, I saw clearly when officially spiritual people were "acting" spiritual. I saw clearly when spirituality was being molded and manipulated to fit a formula as pat and artificial as many movies of the week. This artificial piety disturbed me deeply. Spirituality, as I myself understood it, was quite different from what I saw being presented as "spiritual." Being a writer, I finally had to write about this disturbing dissonance. The result is this book. In it, I have tried to articulate my artist's eye view of spirituality, grounded in my own experience of creating, creation, and the Great Creator— artist *nonpareil*.

You may not find the book you hold in your hands very spiritual—but you'll probably find it spirited. I've tried not to censor my perceptions of the spiritual path, so you will notice the bumps—and some of the grinds. I've included some of my own spiritual lingerie that I call "un-poems," rhymed lyrics I often use to clarify my thoughts. Where they seemed relevant, I left them in the text.

And so you will find lyrics, short essays, tiny creative projects, quizzes, questions, and a potpourri of writing exercises and experiments. You will not find a curriculum. God is not a lesson plan or an intellectual construct. God is not one more thing at which to do well. God is someone or something we meet, each in our own *creative* way.

JULIA CAMERON

BLIND DATE

Most of us don't know where to start with God. We've got a lot of excess baggage and expectations and "God As Told to Us By" and it can feel an awful lot like a Blind Date— the kind you see in those vintage romantic comedies where everybody knows he's the right guy or she's the right girl . . . except the one resisting the date.

The trick with God—just like with Blind Dates—is to suit up and show up. Who knows? God might turn out to be tall and handsome. Or blond and curvy. Someone you might really like. Somebody you can actually talk to and go salsa dancing with. Somebody who gets your jokes and likes the same terrible Japanese monster movies that you do.

The point is that until you try to meet God, you aren't going to know. If your earphones are unspooling the "Here's what God is like" tapes of everybody else, the Spiritual Big Cheeses, you might miss God disguised as the nice trash man who takes your extra load of stuff without making you phone in to bureaucracy hell for another truck and driver. You might miss God as the red-winged black-bird or the shiny river stone. You might miss God, period.

Much of what you learn about God in this country can sound a lot like a military training film, very stern and authoritarian. The message runs along the lines of "God is no laughing matter." I'm not so sure about that. I think God might have a pretty good sense of humor. Look at octopuses, for example. And baboons, with those hilarious bright red asses. Yes, sometimes I think we are the ones who are grim and God is just pacing around cloud nine, waiting for us to lighten up a little. It's possible.

If God is very "serious" to you, you may want to explore just why. Is it God or your conditioning? A bad experience with God, as in dating, can leave you soured.

EXPERIMENT:

The world of Spirit is open to all who seek it. "My Father's house has many mansions," taught Christ. Yet, many of us remain locked in the room of our childhood. As adults, we may be stifled by our unconscious acceptance of a God concept we have long since outgrown. The following questions are aimed at clarifying God as you understand God. Take a pen in hand and answer them. Try for a few sentences or more in each.

1. What was your childhood religion, if any?
2. What was the spiritual atmosphere in your home? Believing? Skeptical? Harsh?
3. What did your mother teach you about God?
4. What did your father teach you about God?
5. Describe your childhood God using at least ten adjectives. Who gave you these words?
6. Is this still the God you believe in? Do you believe at all?
7. What is your current concept of God? Find a magazine image or images of this.
8. Describe your ideal God concept using at least twenty adjectives.
9. Write a letter to your childhood God.
10. Set aside a half hour. Take yourself out of the house. Do something small and festive. Walk, window-shop, enjoy a cappuccino. Sit on a park bench. Be alert to encounter God in any form. This is your Blind Date.

CONNECTION

Before our cities were so crushing and our lives so speeded up, evidence of God was everywhere. We quite literally saw God on the wing. The flash of a cardinal high in the pines was like our soul leaping up, connecting to a sense of Divine Order. The heavens and life here below were believed to be connected—and were experienced as being connected.

In the modern world, faith in a higher order of events is an elected altitude. Even one century ago such a belief undergirded our cultural life having its politicizing in "manifest destiny" and its comforting assumptions literally engraved in stone: "Gone to his Maker."

The cruelty and seeming caprice of the seasons—an untimely frost, a drought—showed a higher hand when viewed in faithful hindsight. With cyclicality and renewal, nature tutored us in faith at every turn. Now we are removed from nature and our natural faith has been eroded. Poets and mystics of all spiritual traditions reported ecstatic sightings of God in everyday events. Our rationalism has trained us away from such spiritual receptivity. We now believe in "coincidence," where we once called it "grace."

This we can directly experience and choose to think of such intimate guidance as spiritual—however personal and pragmatic. This flies in the face of much that we've been taught.

In our rational, busy culture, we often believe in a distant God, too large and disembodied to embrace the very universe It created. Blinded by this belief, we distance ourselves from the Divine help that comes to us in a thousand tiny ways. If God's eye is on the sparrow, ours is too distracted to notice the wren.

This year, I am in Los Angeles for film and theater work. I live a scant mile inland from the Pacific Ocean, a fact that informs the neighborhood's weather. Today began bright, blue, and sunny. The sky was an overturned azure bowl. A neighbor's rosebush offered up one perfect bloom, a coral rose so vibrant, it seemed to pulse with energy. Neighbors strolled hand in hand, basking in the perfect day. A corner yard sale did brisk business. I found a fifteen-dollar bargain slant board for bodywork. Now it feels like

I might need it. A chill gray mist has rolled in off the ocean. It drifts through the trees and gardens like smoke. Back east, mid-October, they would be burning leaves. Here the smoking tendrils of damp speak of the quickening of winter weather.

Now the neighbors hurry past, wrapping their scanty sweaters against the chill. The temperature plummeted fifteen degrees in minutes. It's not warm anymore. Tiger Lily, my gold and white cocker spaniel, abandons the garden to come curl snugly by my side. Her merry mood is gone. She's overcast like the sky.

Just like this morning's tricky weather, one's spiritual condition often seems to vary moment by moment and be largely a matter of perception. It is late afternoon in Manhattan and golden light off the Hudson gilds your office windows. The day is winding down and there are a few moments' time to make personal calls. The setting sun fires the ruddy brick buildings below you to rich medieval hues. The city is a cornucopia of people and experiences, a bazaar stuffed with spices. You place your calls but no one's in. They've all managed to escape the office early. The lovely light wanes. Suddenly, you face a lonely walk home to your cramped apartment. "This city is impossible," you hear yourself say, dreading the evening's enforced solitude. You're taking work home again. . . .

Moods turn on a dime. They brighten or darken our

days. Somehow we must find a spiritual perspective that both honors and ignores them.

As large and troubled as the modern world may be, we are not without power and dignity. In moments when we feel humiliated and overwhelmed, we can choose humor and humility instead of nursing our wounded pride. Instead of asking "Don't they know who I am?" we can take the time to remember who we are. Loving what we love helps us to remember we are lovable. Then we know that, as small as we feel, we are connected to something much larger than ourselves.

EXERCISE:

The world is meant to be savored. It is filled with exquisite delights. This earth is the body of God, as we are. By savoring the delights of this earth, we connect to the divinity that flows through it and through us. Sight leads to insight. Hearing leads to being here. Touching puts us in touch. Scent brings us to our senses.

Please list fifty particular things that you savor. Focusing on what we love in creation, we glimpse what we can love in the Great Creator.

1. Elberta's green chili stew
2. Hollyhocks blooming against an adobe wall
3. Gardenias
4. Map stores
5. Tchaikovsky's "Romeo and Juliet"
6. Etc. . . .

CONSCIOUS
CONTACT

I love the term Conscious Contact for trying to live with spiritual awareness. I know other terms like "practicing the presence," but I always feel the presence doesn't need me to practice. The term Conscious Contact, on the other hand, gives me a sense of wonder like that feeling that swept across Truffaut's beautiful face in *Close Encounters of the Third Kind*. You remember the look: wonder and excitement as he heard the faint celestial message coming back. Contact! And then, when the mother craft came and they all stood there . . .

To me, the term Conscious Contact has a tingly back-of-the-neck magic to it. "Wow. God's here!" I do feel that way sometimes when I watch something fall perfectly and exquisitely into place. I do think, "Ah, divine timing!" X met Y because they both "happened to be" *is* like watching spaceships dock. So, yes, Conscious Contact is my favorite term because there is a lightness and magic about it. A sense that getting in touch with God doesn't need to be all spiritual sit-ups and hard work. That it might be as easy as thinking, "Oh, yes, God." Or even "Hi, God." Like tagging base with mission control. "God, this is Julia. Are you there?"

To be honest, I experience different amounts and kinds of God being "there." Sometimes it is the arm-around-my-shoulder buddy God, like John Glenn being walked across the tarmac to the craft. That palpable sense of God is great—when it happens. And it sometimes does.

My least favorite form of Conscious Contact is what I call "God from Houston." The guidance is still there, but it's disembodied. The arm around the shoulder is gone. Now it's the NASA control aspect of God. You know: "Turn the spacecraft completely upside down. It will be okay. We're watching you from down here. Good luck, John. . . ." I once had five years of that. Yuck!

I believe all of us experience many forms of contact. We just need to be open to them. Sometimes it's the wonder kind. Even the most grown-up grown-up watches a puppy being born and gets the feeling of kids on the staircase watching Santa at work. You can't watch a birth and not think, "This is incredible. . . ." (Or, if you can, I don't want to meet you, you're scary.)

Several years ago, walking on an ordinary afternoon, I suddenly saw the ordinary world around me lit by spiritual radiance. This is what I saw:

JERUSALEM IS WALKING
IN THIS WORLD

This is great happiness.
The air is silk.
There is milk in the looks
That come from strangers.
I could not be happier
If I were bread and you could eat me.
Joy is dangerous.
It fills me with secrets.
"Yes" hisses in my veins.
The pains I take to hide myself
Are sheer as glass.
Surely this will pass,
The wind like kisses,
The music in the soup,
The group of trees,
Laughing as I say their names.

It is all hosanna
It is all prayer.

Jerusalem is walking in this world.
Jerusalem is walking in this world.

I think we are all mystics, but we just forget that or think God speaks only to "special people." That's nonsense.

Conscious Contact can be made through prayer, through song, through meditation, through writing, through walking, through dancing, through drawing, through baking a loaf of bread, through any activity done carefully and consciously with the presence of God held loosely in mind.

EXPERIMENT:

For the next week, try playing with diverse forms of conscious contact, one a day. For example:

1. A twenty-minute walk
2. A letter to God
3. Twenty minutes of sitting meditation
4. Baking something
5. Singing a hymn
6. Reciting small, set prayers throughout the day,

"Thy will be done," "Show Yourself to me,"
"Guide me"

7. Dancing to drum music

At week's end, take time to record what gave you a feeling of well-being.

PRAYER

⌒

Lovers say, "Talk to me." We speak of the love of God. We speak in many spiritual traditions of God as the beloved, and yet when we think of talking to God we find ourselves freezing into the formality of prayer. Lovers use their own words to speak their heart, yet often when we pray we reach for a "great prayer." Like the lover who sends a Shakespearean sonnet or finds the Hallmark card closest to his own sentiment, we often address God as through a filter, or, perhaps better, an interpreter. Maybe it's time we spoke to God more candidly.

The great prayers offer us a glimpse or a view from their saint's spiritual altitude. We may aspire to that altitude, even occasionally achieve it, but more often we might do well to try speaking from our own personal height. And mine is sometimes short.

In 12-Step programs, members are taught to pray "only for the knowledge of God's will for us and the power to carry it out." Intended as an antidote to "gimme-gimme" prayers, this guidance opens the door for God to better direct the seeker's life. Unwittingly, this proviso may sometimes create a barrier to knowing God. If personal needs and problems are not taken up in prayer, how can a working partnership be forged?

Belief in a distant God creates in the believer a feeling of powerlessness and oppression. Simultaneously, it creates a feeling of resentment. "Why," we ask, "didn't God do something about the Holocaust? Or poverty? Or the violence in inner cities?" If these things are blamed on God, we're off the hook. We do not need to ask "What can we do?"

A distant God, however alienating, is a convenient God. How much more troublesome and demanding is the notion that God is eminent, available to us in all times and all circumstances—always ready to fuel and guide our endeavors no matter how small or large. There is no evading responsibility with a God so close, so personal, and so available. In every circumstance, at every turn, such a God may be called upon for insight, inspiration, and right action. Is it any wonder we prefer the idea of a distant God that must be cajoled and flattered?

If we believe in such a capricious, withholding, or indifferent deity, a God of arrogance, we can easily feel that our dreams and desires are ungodly. Viewing life in Gerard Manley Hopkins's terms, as "charged with the grandeur of God," we begin to approach a form of spirituality that encounters God not as the distant creator but as the indwelling creative force of which we ourselves are a manifestation, and which we ourselves as creators continue to manifest. Dylan Thomas's "force that through the green fuse drives the flower" works through all of us.

God's will and our own are not necessarily at opposite ends of the table, but until we open a dialogue with God, until we begin a genuine conversation, we are like partners in an empty marriage, afraid to air our views. We can tell God what we want, we can tell God what we don't want, and we can fight about it some of the time. It may sound sacrilegious, but it's a lot like having sex. You've *got* to communicate.

"For the first ten years of my sobriety, I prayed only for knowledge of God's will and the power to carry it out," says Thomas. "I found that, as a result, I was keeping my true goals and dreams a secret both from God and myself. Tentatively, feeling like a heretic, I began to pray for help with what I needed and wanted as well as for the knowledge of God's will for me and the power to carry it out. Immediately, I felt a heightened sense of spiritual companionship. As my prayers were answered, I began to feel security that God did, in fact, care for me."

"Thank-you" is a potent prayer. Gratitude is a heightened and receptive spiritual state. Affirmative prayers in which we thank God for blessing we have yet to receive is a potent way of reinforcing faith.

"I am guided. I am protected," we pray—and we are.

Prayer is talking to God. We can talk in a whisper. We can talk in a shout. We can talk body language. We can talk in pictures. We can talk through music. We can talk through rhyme. What matters is less how we talk than that we talk. "Goddammit, I pray badly" is a perfect prayer. "My God, my God, why have You forsaken me?" is what Jesus prayed. He did not mince words.

EXPERIMENT:

Because prayer is talking to God, depending on your concept of God, such conversation can be easy or difficult. Just as many of us unconsciously cling to outmoded concepts of God, we cling, too, to outmoded concepts of prayer. Take pen in hand and examine your own attitudes. Again, go for more than "yes" or "no." Get to the "why?" and "why not?" if you can.

1. Do you believe in prayer?
2. What kind of prayer do you believe in?
3. Do you have a favorite prayer?

4. Have you ever written a prayer of your own?

5. Is there a prayer you admire? Which one? Why?

6. Have you tried prayers of gratitude?

7. Have you tried prayers of praise?

8. Do you pray for your friends? Why or why not?

9. Do you pray for help with specific difficulties or goals?

10. Do you pray for guidance? How?

11. Did you have a favorite childhood prayer? Write it out. What do you like about it?

12. Did you have a favorite hymn or sung prayer? Sing it out. Note what it does.

13. Do you have a favorite hymn now?

14. Have you experimented with walking and praying? Try a twenty-minute prayer walk.

15. Write a prayer for yourself as if you were your most cherished friend.

CATCH-UP BALL

When I was in grammar school, we had jokes with punch lines like this one: "Were you standing behind the door when God passed out brains?" Maybe that's where so many of us got the idea that spiritually we were a little slow and had to play Catch-up Ball. Of course, the notion of original sin didn't help much either—the concept that you are fundamentally flawed tends to promote what therapists now call low self-esteem.

So there we are, seriously flawed and dumb enough to be in the wrong place when God was handing out the goodies. Dumb enough, we might fear, to *still* be in the wrong place when God is handing out the goodies. If you believe in original sin, it's a short hop to believing in original mistake. Original mistake goes something like this:

"I turned left instead of right, so I never met my soul mate."

"I went north instead of south, so I ended up at the wrong job."

"I've been making errors like this ever since, and it's no wonder God can't find me to hand out the goodies."

This is an interesting catch-22. We have faith in God but not in ourselves. We believe that God could and would help us but that we've botched it somehow. As a result, we have to play Catch-up Ball, trying to come from behind and somehow make up our losses. The idea that we might actually be right on schedule, in the right place at the right time, doesn't come naturally when you've got low spiritual self-worth (which is encouraged by the scolding tone of some spiritual teachers). It's as if we believe that yes, we *were* behind that door. In fact, we still are. It's the bottom of the ninth and we're about to let down the team. If we have faith in anything, we have faith in that. Is it any wonder we have a hard time stepping up to the plate? We feel like Walter in the classic film *The Secret Life of Walter Mitty*—small and beleaguered, henpecked, and harassed. We forget that even Walter got his happy ending and that we may also get ours.

EXPERIMENT:

Many of us feel alienated from God because we find something that we did—or didn't do—unacceptable, unforgivable. Often this is unconscious. We drift away from God as we might drift away from a friend toward whom we have an unspoken resentment or unshared secret. Take pen in hand and do a little archaeological digging.

1. Do you have a chronic feeling of playing catch-up ball?
2. Do you have any historical mistake that you blame for ruining your life?
3. Did you ask God to undo it?
4. Would you ask God to undo it?
5. What would symbolize being caught up to you? Can you take one step toward this?

REST

"Rest" is a musical term, a tiny breather built into the melodic structure, giving the beauty of the melody a little space to expand in consciousness. "Rest" is also a spiritual term. We are told to "rest in our faith," "rest in our Christ consciousness," "rest in the loving arms of the Lord." We usually take such admonitions to be metaphorical. We hear them as though they said "focus." We are accustomed to thinking of spirituality as hard work, and the idea that it might not be is foreign to us.

"Rest in the Lord" means "stop trying." Instead of reaching to a distant God, allow a more intimate one. Stop giving God your attention. Let God give you some attention. Receive.

Prayers of petition, a position of supplication—these we understand. The idea of God as a loving heart or hearth, the notion of a spiritual relationship without effort—this takes a little getting used to.

Velocity is addictive and velocity for the sake of velocity is a constant temptation. If it takes discipline to work, it also takes discipline not to work, to allow the water level to rise until action becomes again the natural spilling forth of inner fullness. There is a cyclicality to life, a recognizable on-off pulse. When we go with this current, we experience a sense of rightness. When we force action, we experience strain. And yet, forcing action can be more comfortable and familiar than allowing fruitful ambiguity. Ambiguity frequently breeds anxiety, and this uncomfortable anxiety in turn catalyzes new directions. The ability to endure ambiguity is a learned skill. As an artist, I have learned that every play, novel, and book contains a dark and murky period that must be worked through. The trick is to just show up, even when there is no apparent gain. Slowing down, showing up, and *listening* to the unfolding work *eventually* puts things right. This is akin to meditation.

One of the reasons many of us avoid meditation is that we think of it as work—and work we may not do perfectly. What if we didn't have to do it perfectly? What if we didn't have to "do" it at all? What if we could rest—and let God do the rest?

There are some terms that are useful here. One often-used phrase is "practicing the presence." Practicing the presence is just that, thinking "Oh, yes, God" and doing nothing further about it. This is a form of remembering God is a presence, like air. We forget about air and we forget about God. When we remember them, they are everywhere, ordinary and miraculous.

Another phrase for spiritual ease is "taking a quiet time." The only active thing we need to do is "take" the time. The quiet does the rest.

It is one of the gifts of great spiritual teachers to make things simple. It is one of the gifts of their followers to complicate them again. Often we need to scrape away the accumulated complications of a master's message in order to hear the kernel of what they said. Christ advised us to "become as little children." Children play and children rest—two concepts foreign to most of the current thinking regarding spirituality. And yet, some of the most sweetly successful spiritual lives are grounded in precisely those principles.

EXPERIMENT:

Ours is a busy and driven world. Spirituality can easily become one more agenda. Being "spiritual" can be an attribute to list in the personals. We try so hard that it's trying. This week, expand your notion of what is spiritual to include a little more breathing room. Listen to a great Broadway show instead of a chant album. Go to a comedy instead of a politically correct art movie. Read a great mystery instead of a self-help book like this one. Instead of getting up an hour earlier, go to bed an hour earlier. Instead of tackling more, try tackling less. Let God work on you instead of you working on God. You will notice there is no official exercise, except to consciously choose something and record the results.

VERY SPIRITUAL
PEOPLE

One of my favorite characters in our national creative consciousness is Church Lady from *Saturday Night Live*. Her piety masked rigid judgment. We all knew it and laughed. She struck our funny bone because we recognized the pettiness of a village gossip behind a spiritual façade. In my experience, a very spiritual demeanor *often* masks pettiness and judgment. I get pretty uncomfortable around Very Spiritual People. You know the kind that I mean. They talk in low, sweet, soft, gentle monotone voices until you want to pinch them or tickle them or hit them with a baseball bat. No matter how sweet and calm they say they are—and they usually do tell you that when they've got a minute— I still feel something that feels a lot like rage and control seeping out.

You know how it goes. You tell them that you're upset about something and they act like you should be able to transcend it. They act really sad, like you're being really petty or maybe you're just a huge spiritual disappointment to them. They get this kind of sad, wise, all-knowing look on their face like they're a little hurt by your lack of altitude. Like they had expected something better from you . . . something like them, for example.

You can tell when you've met one of these officially spiritual types because they won't laugh no matter what. At best they may smile thinly. To them, God is no laughing matter—although a lot of the stuff they do themselves is pretty funny, if you ask me.

Sometimes when you talk to them, Very Spiritual People close their eyes and sort of nod sagely as if they were on heroin. They do this in lots of situations where they are being officially spiritual. You're at a spiritual talk, for example, or a concert, and all of a sudden, whoops, there go the eyes and now they're rocking back and forth a little in this kind of embarrassing way. Maybe I'm just a prude. But the rocking and moaning bit looks a little to me like the thing Meg Ryan did in that café in *When Harry Met Sally.* Very Spiritual People are very serious about being very spiritual.

Maybe this is a terrible thing to say, but I actually think that Very Spiritual People are pretty mean and controlling and passive-aggressive. (Of course, even thinking that means

I am not spiritual.) It's something about the way they act, like they are God's Nazi enforcers. The way they seem to want you to tiptoe and toe the line and behave. That quiet little voice they use always sounds pretty fake to me and just sounds, well, furious. Sometimes they sort of hiss in a spiritual way.

"You can't do that here . . ." and then going all sweetie-pie, "now, can you?"

Very Spiritual People scare me to death. And they like to make God and spirituality *very* scary. If you do it wrong, watch *out!* They act like they've got a lock on it. They know the secrets. It's kind of like a spiritual clubhouse. You can't get in without the secret handshake. They've got God's private number and you have to go through the operator. Very Spiritual People just hate it when you think you can talk to God all by yourself. Like the minions guarding the hideout in *The Dark Crystal*, they seem to feel:

HIGHER REALMS

You must be careful in things of the spirit
To be sure you're really near it.
To be sure you're on the mark
No mere beginner filled with luck
Can read the signs quite clear enough
To find the trail that leads straight to the grail.

You have to be an initiate!
You've got spiritual teeth to cut!
As above, so below, but there is still red tape, you know!
You need a keen sense of bureaucracy!
Higher realms aren't a democracy!

You can't just rush in willy-nilly,
Why, the very idea is silly.
You've got to pay your dues, and we're who choose.

EXPLORE:

These questions may be volatile. Write in detail to discover *why*.

1. Do you know any people who are officially "very spiritual"?
2. Are you officially "very spiritual"? How so?
3. Do you see being "very spiritual" as a form of snobbery? Explore this on the page.
4. Who do you know who is genuinely spiritual? Describe them. What are your favorite traits?
5. What have you done that expresses your genuine spiritual values? List at least ten things.

SPIRITUAL CELLULITE

During my years as an East Coast writer living dead center in Hollywood, I often felt like a plain brown wren—or perhaps a pretty little finch darting amid the loud and colorful peacocks and parrots. Why couldn't I look like Pamela Anderson *and* write, I sometimes wondered, when I found myself standing in a room full of tall, artificially statuesque blondes, women so buffed they might have been made of plastic—and probably were. It is easy to convince yourself you have terrible cellulite when you are standing next to someone so *purrfect*. Spiritually, I can have exactly the same issue. I think a lot of us can. I've never felt I had a very buff spirituality. I've always had problems with doing the "proper" spiritual sit-ups and so I have just sort of figured I had to live with my Spiritual Cellulite and not try for God's Pinup Girl of the Month.

For example, I hate going to the gym for my physical body, so I go for long walks and bike rides. That's a good time for spiritual check-in, and I do seem to hear a lot of great advice from Something when I am outside and moving. On the other hand, I have always felt it would be more spiritually acceptable if I were getting the advice when I was inside and not moving, but sitting meditation has never been my long suit, unless you count sitting down every morning and doing my Morning Pages, three pages of longhand writing, where I seem to get my spiritual marching orders of the day. I have found that's an effective form of meditation for me, but I am sure it's cheating to be writing my thoughts down instead of just letting them glide by like clouds.

I have had people tell me things like "I'm very spiritual, Julia," and I have found it a little terrifying, like having someone slide up and say "Don't I have spectacular legs?" when I am trying on a swimming suit and thinking the opposite. Now, maybe this is false modesty on my part, but maybe it's just plain modesty. And what does "very spiritual" mean?

The people I know who are actually very spiritual don't talk about it much. They seem to be sort of festive and kind and interested in other people and then later—sometimes much later—you find they get up early and pray, or they keep a little stash of spiritual reading by the bed, or even in the glove compartment. They don't tell me they are "very spiritual" and they probably don't think they are.

Now, when I talk about Spiritual Cellulite, I am not saying that I think we're supposed to sit around and examine ourselves like Miss Tennessee right before we go out on the runway for the swimsuit competition. No. What I am saying is that maybe a few spiritual lumps and tiny little bulges are normal and we should all just go swimming anyway.

Often when I hear people talk about their spiritual practice, I think the word "practice" got left out. I get intimidated because they seem to do it so perfectly. And so much. And so often. It gets to sound like doing the "right" kind of crunch, so that their spiritual abs get a great cut. They talk about their sponsor, or their spiritual counselor, or their guru like they've just joined Radu's in Manhattan, the one where all the supermodels work out. They have this air of spiritual superiority, as if your regular old sit-up doesn't really cut it. Supermodel spirituality can make me feel as rotten as trying on my Speedo suit next to their thong bikini. And I do think that some people wear their spiritual-persuasion sweatshirt just like a Radu T-shirt.

There's something about spiritual competition that strikes me as a non sequitur. Narcissism and ego in the name of spiritual growth seems precisely like narcissism and ego in the name of anything else—a little self-absorbed and exhausting. Then, too, there's something a little humorless about always having to scramble for the spiritual high ground of "my way is right." It reminds me of trying to get great at the climbing wall or learn the new machine so you don't have to admit that you're still doing the old kind of presses.

Sometimes when people start to tell me how spiritually buff they are, how many retreats they have been on and how long they can meditate at a crack, I feel like we're playing a game of who can swim the longest underwater. It seems that the number of laps counts more than the swimming, like the serious goggles might keep you from noticing the pretty little sparkles in the pool. Also, if you can't ever flip over on your back and float for a minute, how do you notice how silky the water feels and how the sky is an azurine bowl and you feel sort of nice?

It seems to me that sometimes we can get so busy doing our spiritual aerobics that we don't notice the light in the trees and feel of the sun on our skin, because we are speed-walking instead of ever going out for a stroll. If we're always trying to get better, where is there a minute for "good enough" or even "this is okay for now"? A few extra ounces or pounds maybe, but okay?

SPIRITUAL CELLULITE

All of us have our flaws
But spiritual cellulite is the cause

Of such self-loathing and despair
You'd think we had torn underwear.
"I'm not getting anywhere"
Seems to be our constant prayer.
We stare into our spiritual mirror
Pinching at our spiritual rear.

EXERCISE:

Many of us suffer from spiritual low self-worth. We harbor feelings of unworthiness that prevent us from even trying for greater spiritual contact.

Explore these questions in writing, then choose an action from part two or devise a comparable action of your own.

1. Do you beat yourself up about how unspiritual you are?
2. Do you believe that other people "do" their spirituality better? Who? Why?
3. Do you feel you're lousy at prayer?
4. Does your meditation practice seem shabby?
5. Has it ever occurred to you to make your spiritual practice something you enjoy?

Part Two:
You could:

Pray and dance.
Pray and walk.
Pray and bike.

You could:

Pray and sing.
Pray and paint.
Pray and take a good, hot bath.

SPIRITUAL EXPERTS —
HOW MANY ANGELS
CAN DANCE IN
THIS JOINT?

One of the things Very Spiritual People sometimes like to do is get into God as a game of Trivial Pursuit. They like to be "God experts" and they know all the tiny little facts about God that might trip you up if you just wanted to go over and say "Hi, God" at the garden fence.

In their world, God doesn't go over to the garden fence. In their world God lives at the center of the maze and you can get to God only if you know all the secret handshakes and passageways and passwords.

I call these people Spiritual Experts, and you'll know when you meet one. Let's say you tell them you think there might be angels. And you might have—whoops! Well, they know exactly all about angels, like they've spent nine or ten years in angel seminars where the types of angels and their jobs are all very carefully explained. So, if you say "Maybe an angel helped me," they'll be like "Maybe an M-7 helped you"—whatever an M-7 is. Or they might say "No, M-7s never work on your level."

In other words, their theory of how it is supposed to work is a lot more important than whatever your experience was. They're a little like expert bird-watchers. You say, "There was this pretty little yellow bird, maybe a finch or a canary or something, and it came to sit on the windowsill while I was writing. . . ." And, watch out, you've pressed their play button.

"It couldn't have been a finch or canary. It might have been a yellow-bellied spirit obscurus."

"Oh, you mean a little angel?"

Then they sniff, like that's a word that only plebes would use.

SPIRITUAL EXPERTS

Maybe it makes me an underachiever
But I can't stomach the kind of believer
Who talks like an expert on spiritual matters.
Is it just me, do they sound like mad hatters?
How many angels dance on a pin?
How many non-kosher will Yahweh let in?
How many Novenas will open the gate?
How much of the Torah lends spiritual weight?

Spiritual experts can't seem to agree,
I just hope they don't starting fighting with me.

One of the things you will notice pretty quickly about the Spiritual Experts club is that it feels a lot like any other special club. First of all, it's hard to get in, and once you do, the main fun they seem to have there is keeping everybody else out. Let's say you think so-and-so is interesting. "No, no, not a real expert!"

Now, most of the people in the Spiritual Experts club are boys. I mean men. There are a few girls in it, but usually either they talk like the men or they risk getting tossed out. Unless they are old and saintly and remind the men of Grandma, like Mother Teresa. Or maybe they are sort of a spiritual dish like Marianne Williamson. Mostly, though, the ones who get in cut their hair like ex-nuns and act very serious and a little mean.

I remember meeting one of those. She was wearing her ex-nun outfit—a boxy little suit and short hair—and I looked kind of like Rita Hayworth in *Gilda*. (Even if I do say so myself.) Well, we were both supposed to be lecturing on spirituality and she kind of looked me up and down and hissed—I mean *hissed*—"Why can't you dress like the rest of us?"

"Because I don't want to," I told her. She did not want to hear that. It seemed to make her even madder and nastier than usual. She whipped out there and scolded that audience just the way Sister Very Nasty used to when I was little. According to her, they were really botching their lessons. And she *knew* . . . Lou Gosset's fanatical drill sergeant in *An Officer and a Gentleman* had nothing on her.

She whipped right into the Sister Very Nasty version, which uses a lot of sarcasm and cruelty "for your own good." This version is all about lessons, and how you are doing them wrong. In this version, God is really not very fond of us. It's like He thinks we are social climbers trying to get to Him and He can see right through us and so can Sister Very Nasty.

Another kind of serious is what I call "mysterious serious." You know who practices this one. (Or, at least, he's the best at practicing this one.)

One of the things that people in the Spiritual Experts club like to do is get very serious. They get serious faster than Mario Andretti can spit. Just try having a little fun. Watch out. They'll whip out some version of serious. I've seen some pretty fancy ones. "Of course you're frivolous! Artists are only at Level Five, spirtually." My theory is that since some of them don't write their own books, they get pretty defensive around people who do.

E X E R C I S E :

Playing "expert" is often a way that people—ourselves included—may cope with a difficult emotion. It is also a technique people may use to create a power imbalance, making themselves feel "one up." Most of us do this occasionally; some people do it chronically.

Write these answers and share them with a very good-humored friend.

1. Do you play spiritual expert? About what? With whom? How often?
2. When someone else plays spiritual expert, do you get mad? Annoyed? Alienated? Who? When?
3. Do you use spiritual expert as a defense mechanism against intimacy? Do you delver spiritual lectures to friends in pain?
4. Do you recognize when the spiritual-expert mechanism is being used to create distance?
5. Do you know any spiritual teachers who do not play expert? Who?

EXERCISE:

Contact with God is a personal matter. Contact with a religious organization can have the same social pecking order as any other human organization; you will discover both camaraderie and snobbery.

Write these answers and share them with a compassionate friend.

1. Do you recognize when you are being excluded spiritually?
2. Do you yourself exclude people?
3. Do you make any effort to include others in your spirituality?
4. Are you able to share the spirituality of others?
5. What spiritual tradition other than your own do you appreciate?

FAITH

Maybe I've watched one too many Vegas comedians whip up a crowd too many times not to think that spiritual snake oil isn't just the same old show-business snake oil being sold in the same old showbiz "over-the-top" way. Take the little matter of faith . . .

I think faith is overrated. At the very least, it's oversold. We are told we need more faith, as though if we find a bolt of this rare and silken cloth, then everything will become really wonderful. "Just have more faith," we are often advised. I don't know anybody I trust who thinks they have enough faith. It's the spiritual equivalent of being skinny. We all think we could be a little more so.

I'm not being quite accurate. I do know a few people—and I have actually heard quite a few more—who are a little vain about the amount of faith they have. Sometimes they almost seem to gloat about it. "I'm very spiritual," they actually say. I keep waiting for them to get their turn in the barrel. When times get rough for them, their faith seems low too. Faith is a little like chocolate. A little is great, but there's never enough, and sooner or later you're going to run dangerously low.

"You have so much faith," I am sometimes told, usually by someone who thinks one of my creative endeavors—putting on a musical, for example, or publishing a crime novel—looks risky or scary.

"Enough faith?" I think. "Are you out of your mind? Look at the gas tank. The needle's near empty! I just do things anyhow!"

"I just do things anyhow" is a pretty good definition of a working faith. As in "I'm scared to death about actually committing to this marriage . . . the new job . . . bringing up a new puppy . . . moving to L.A., but I just do it anyhow."

Does this mean that faith is about walking blindfolded off cliffs? In the Tarot deck, yes. That is exactly what the Fool card is doing. The Fool is probably God's favorite card. Most of the great saints have been tremendous fools—St. Joan, Mother Teresa, Cesar Chavez, and Martin Luther King, to name a few.

They've undertaken great missions based on listening to the still, small voice that egged them on. People thought they were crazy, and maybe they were. They certainly took big and crazy-looking risks. But was there really a risk? Maybe they were much more secure than the rest of us because they weren't hedging their bets and dangling over the chasm of rationality, doubt on one side, faith on the other, and a hand grabbing wildly at each.

Saints commit. They practice the Nike ad: "Just do it." This is how they got things done. Needless to say (I hope), we are not saints and our commitments don't have to be those of Butch and Sundance, jumping off the cliff. (They just feel that way.) The cliff may be only a coffee table after all.

EXERCISE:

Many of us have difficulty believing in the action of Spirit in our lives because we have difficulty believing we are worthy of Spirit's help. Often we have lurking subconscious beliefs about our own deservedness. Consciously, we know better. But unconsciously, we harbor feelings of low spiritual self-worth. What follows is a three-part exercise:

Step One: Writing very rapidly, complete the phrase:

"The reason I don't deserve spiritual help is . . ."

Moving your hand as quickly as possible, do it ten times. What pops up may surprise and dismay you.

"I'm divorced," your unconscious may blurt out.

"I'm a lapsed Catholic."

"I had an abortion."

"I slapped my kid."

And now write a positive affirmation that contradicts your negative belief.

"I am divorced but worthy of God's love."

"I am a spiritual being despite leaving the Catholic Church."

"God loves and accepts me and my choices."

"I am a wise and compassionate parent."

Step Two: Write a letter to God, the Universe, your higher self, or the higher forces, laying out the areas in which you feel bad. Ask for the grace to forgive yourself, to accept forgiveness, and to receive healing and support. If possible, go to a beautiful natural spot. Read the letter aloud. Then burn it, shred it, bury it.

Step Three: If fear is "false evidence appearing real," a lack of faith is often real evidence appearing false. In order to experience faith, we must draw to consciousness evidence of difficult situations successfully resolved.

This is an "ah-hah!" list. It tells us "I *did* receive help, support, guidance, and successful resolution." Take pen in hand again and list ten situations in which you received help, support, guidance, and resolution.

BULLIES

I remember sitting at a Hollywood dinner, listening in fascinated horror one night as an actor regaled the dinner guests with a story of nearly dying by drowning while filming a beach combat scene in which the director bullied cast and crew into take after take as the tide was rising. Of course, this bullying was done in the name of Art. It was still just bullying. Bullies in the name of spirituality are really still just bullies. You're not supposed to know this and they will do their level best to keep you from figuring it out. Spiritual bullies have a whole bag of tricks that they use to keep you off center. Here are just a few of them:

1. The this-is-very-mysterious trick
You will know that this trick is being used whenever a speaker starts to talk down to you. And does it in a very

complicated and hard-to-follow way. Like he just smoked a lot of great Moroccan hash. Speakers who are using this trick don't really care about communicating with you. They care about talking. You're incidental. What they want is for you to feel lucky enough to have listened to them and, if their barely comprehensible theories make your head spin, you're supposed to understand that this means you are shallow and they are deep and you just don't get it. You are not supposed to stand up and shout "So, Bebop, does this all boil down to sound body sound mind, or vice versa?" Bebop does not want you to make it easy. That's why he sounds mysterious and you might even think spurious. Am I the only one who thinks of Eddie Albert as the smarmy peddler in *Oklahoma!*, or Fisher Stevens in the *Short Circuit* series, selling and seducing his way door to door and state to state—a study in double-talking snake oil sincerity—all delivered in an accent as greasily smooth as the elixir such peddlers sell?

2. The this-is-serious trick

When a teacher is using the this-is-serious trick, he will act like he's the spiritual equivalent of Mensa. He and Buddha might share this altitude. His theories will also be complicated, but not so much in that hazy hashish way, more in a mazelike brainbuster way. Clever. He wants you to say "Isn't this a-mazing!"—emphasis on the *maze*. He will talk about "maps of consciousness" as if God is a continent only he can explore, terra incognita to the rest of us. He wants you to know you are dealing with Mr. Wizard (think of Peter Sellers in *Dr. Strangelove*). His theories are all about being smart, and so they are really all about your head and his head. His head might even look a little like a spiritual lightbulb. That's how bright he is.

3. The this-makes-me-furious trick

This is the trick that usually gets used by teachers with a Sister-Very-Nasty persona. These teachers use scorn and sarcasm to make you feel like spiritual midgets. They try to shame you about your spiritual altitude as if they were intellectual versions of Church Lady and you're a dumb plebe. They sort of mock their listeners. They use terms like "You may *even* believe such-and-such" or "If I were your spiritual adviser, I'd say . . ." Watch out!

4. The airy-fairy trick

This trick is being used when the teacher stares into space a lot, like Higher Beings are there but you can't see them. (Think of Noel Coward talking to his invisible wife in *Blithe Spirit*.) The game here is you're AM and I'm FM, so I will tell you about higher realms because you couldn't get there with an escalator. If you ask these speakers a question, they look sad that you aren't evolved enough to understand their answer.

5. The shell-game trick

This trick starts when the teacher is selling some new technology and wants you in on the ground level so he can maximize your profit. Questions like "What does the gizmo really do?" are treated like they are beside the point and then you get handed five hundred pages of fine print, explaining that the gizmo was tested on three people once. (The movie archetypes for this one are *Repo Man*, and, of course, *The Sting*.)

6. The let-me-sell-you-this-bridge trick

This trick is being used when the teacher says something peppy and then waits for your response like you're at a college pep rally. "Do we love God? Do we want higher consciousness?" this speaker shouts. You might wonder if God is a Ford or Chevy being sold this way. You might wonder if the speaker ever met Elmer Gantry.

EXERCISE:

One of the most controversial episodes in the New Testament is the recounting of Christ chasing the money changers out of the temple. My Lord! The Lord has lost His temper! Yes, He did, and He did so because people were being bullied and extorted in the name of spirituality. It is an unfortunate fact that charismatic spiritual leaders may also become bullies. A bully asks that you surrender your spiritual autonomy and do as you are told. Whenever we are bullied in *any* area of our lives, our spiritual dignity is being ignored. Calling a bully a bully is the first step toward restoring our balanced autonomy. Taking an independent action in the direction you were bullied out of is the second step.

Take pen in hand. Create three columns. In column one, list those who have bullied you—financially, creatively, sexually—in whatever form. In column two, identify what they were bullying you out of. For example, a spiritual teacher who tells you that you cannot trust yourself and your perceptions is bullying you out of following your unique and personal intuition, the "still, small voice" within. In column three, as an antidote, you might try taking a small step in the direction your intuition has been urging. If you have been medically bullied, you may be talked out of your sense of personal guidance regarding your health. You might seek a second opinion, or turn to the Internet and research the condition yourself.

When we have been bullied, especially in the name of spirituality, we may become bullies ourselves and continue in the same vicious cycle. Take pen in hand.

Draw three vertical columns. In column one, list those you may have bullied. In column two, list how and in what way you overran their spiritual autonomy. In column three, list a loving, festive action that you can undertake to support them. Take that action.

EXTREME SKIERS

Both comedy and horror hinge on the element of surprise. The more extreme the surprise, the more comic—or horrifying—the result. As a dramatist on the spirituality circuit, I encountered a lot of extremes that were both comic and horrifying to me. I found some spiritual practices, like living entirely on water and blue-green algae, were so ill-considered that it was a little like watching an old Harold Lloyd movie where he dangled off skyscraper ledges. Others were so risky—pencil-thin, Armani-clad Beverly Hills spiritual seekers trekking in their Bruno Magli shoes on vision quests, alone in snake-infested canyon territory, a privilege for which they paid big bucks—that it was like watching Evil Kanevil try to rocket a motorcycle over a zillion parked cars. Sooner or later, somebody was going to break something. One of the things that's scary about Very Spiritual People is that they can be an awful lot like Extreme Skiers, the kind who jump off cliffs doing wild stunts and then brag about it. Take the extreme yoga crowd. They twist their bodies into wild knots and then suggest you do it if you really want to be spiritual. (What about my back? you may be thinking.) Or the extreme meditation crowd. They recommend meditating for maybe twelve hours a day, and if you don't want to do it or run off and be silent and meditate sixteen hours a day and watch your mind like TV, well then, you are a disappointment. You are just not serious about God.

And why are we supposed to be serious about God? Did God show up and crack the whip? "You there, Annie in Ohio, I see you laughing a lot and frankly it really pisses Me off . . ."

God, who invented kittens and ladybugs as well as cobras and tigers, may have a pretty good emotional keyboard. Maybe we have just been taught to do God in the scary minor keys or the big majestic ones and that can be fine, I am sure, but personally I think there is God in the zippy little cartoon keys also.

But back to the extreme bit. I'm not sure it's such a great idea. I think it might be the spiritual equivalent of the grapefruit-and-one-fig-leaf diet. (That's the one where all you eat is grapefruit until you're so damn skinny you can run around without your fig leaf and still feel groovy.) My theory is that Adam and Eve grabbed those leaves because they had cellulite.

So. The Extreme Skier Crowd of Spirituality likes to get all wound up about how God talks to you better if you go to the ashram and get malnutrition. I think God does talk to you then, but maybe because She's worried. I think when we fast we trigger the Jewish Mother aspect of God—and rightly so.

Another thing I think is that a lot of the fasting and meditating-for-hours bit is really just Type A spirituality. We want to know God, but faster. So, we try to manipulate a little so God's got to talk to us, if only to say "Honey, cut that out!"

I don't know if you've ever gone to an ashram or a New Age spiritual potential center, but I have. They were started with good intentions and the whiff of spiritual superiority necessary to assume the missionary position. The food there is usually Nouvelle Nazi—brown rice and mysterious greens and Tofu Torment with lots of shapeless sauces. The people who actually live there and eat it can get a very funny look in their eyes. They might call it being clear, but I wouldn't let them walk my baby across the street. They're so spiritual, they're not grounded. They're so spiritual that it's hard for them to change the beds and weed the organic garden. They stare into midair a lot, like maybe they're seeing the Holy Ghost. They don't call Him that though. They call it having insights. They have insights and a special patented nonsexual hug they give each other all the time that is kind of embarrassing to watch, like they're linking up all their chakras and rubbing them. Nonsexually, of course. Personally, I think anything that gets them to come back and visit their bodies is a good idea. Yoga can work that way but generally doesn't. It's used to tune out, not tune in.

I happen to know that some of the people who live at these places secretly eat meat. Maybe it's because they've come too close once too often to walking off the cliff. They suddenly get it: "Jesus—are you listening?—I better get grounded." Grounded usually means ground beef. Like "Get me a hamburger at the speed of light." And so they race off secretly on an official ashram mission to the greasy spoon twenty miles away, where they have a hamburger, double fries, and a chocolate malted. This is smart. A lot of the people who teach at the centers do it. Of course, you can try to arrange to have red meat if you already know you need it to stay on the ground, but that can get pretty hilarious and feel an awful lot like a dope deal. "Okay, I've got your (gasp) meat and if you sneak into the kitchen at two A.M. and use a special unholy skillet, then you can eat it if you have to. . . ."

Some of us have to. Many Native American teachers refuse to teach without red meat. They know that powerful energies require grounding. Of course, this belief is regarded as primitive. Give me primitive.

EXPERIMENT:

Moderation is a learned spiritual attitude. Buddha himself went to ascetic extremes before recommending a more temperate approach. For most of us, spiritual growth has the ring of "work" to it. We bring a harsh eye to our spiritual endeavors, always feeling we should do "more" or "better." This self-punishing attitude often dampens our spiritual ardor. Answer the following questions:

1. If you didn't have to do it perfectly, what spiritual practice might you try? List at least three. Try one.
2. What forms of spiritual extremism do you practice? Write about this. What is its appeal to you?
3. What forms of spiritual sweetness could you allow yourself? Listen. Try one.
4. Do you still associate being spiritual with long-suffering martyrdom? List ten ways you are mean or cheap to yourself.
5. Do you appreciate the difference between gentle practice and rigid discipline? What could you adjust? Try it.

EXERCISE:

A spiritual practice is a consecrated activity done regularly and repetitively. We can't do it perfectly. The important thing is that we *do* do it. This is a lesson well learned from my years of writing—just get something down on the page each day, no matter what. In my personal spiritual life, I use several favorite practices.

My primary spiritual practice is the daily writing of Morning Pages. These have been the cornerstone of my spiritual life for nearly two decades. They ground me, center me, open me to guidance, prioritize my day, and stabilize my moods. I have found them to be a wonderful form of meditation for myself, as a hyperactive Westerner. A second favored spiritual practice is a daily walk. Walking is a contemplative activity. It both stills and frees the mind, moving us across the bridge into the Imagic-Nation, where higher forces can speak to us with clarity. *"Solvitur ambulando,"* declared St. Augustine. Answers come to us when we walk.

My third regular spiritual practice is bike riding. The physicality of this practice puts me into my body, where I encounter my true feelings and gain a sense of direction. The choice of a spiritual practice is personal. Some of us revel in chant. Others hear the still, small

voice best in silence. This week, you are experimenting with multiple forms of spiritual practice.

Answer the following questions:

1. What is the best time of day for you to experience
   conscious contact? (For me, it is early morning
   and just before bed.)
2. What form of physical spiritual practice appeals to
   you? Why? Try a *little* of it.
3. Do you find sound or silence conducive to a sense
   of spiritual connection?
4. Have you, or could you, establish any personal
   daily rituals? Choose one one-minute one.
5. What practice seems exotic but appealing to you?
   Try it.

STRUCTURE

Six months ago I moved to Los Angeles for a hopefully brief work-related stay. The days unfurl like bolts of limitless blue silk. Seasons are as discreet as an Armani stripe. I find myself craving structure. In monasteries of every denomination, time is metered out. One rises and prays at a certain hour. One works, prays again, and eats at a certain hour. Next, we have more work, more prayer, another meal, another round of prayer, then bed. The great adventure of a spiritual life is led within the solid gridwork of structure.

Prayer was once a regular part of nearly everyone's life. There was Sunday service, often one at midweek, certainly prayers before meals, usually prayers upon rising and again as we retired. Reading from the Bible or other holy books was often the evening's activity. This was before television, before radio, before surfing the Web.

Our modern lives are structured by our secular activities and not our spiritual ones. We have *Good Morning America* or *The Today Show* in the time slot for prayers upon rising. David Letterman helps us say "amen" to the day.

Unless we consciously build a spiritual structure into our days, we are apt to go without. How are we to remember who we are unless we take the time to remind ourselves?

When we structure spiritual interludes into our day, we are giving spiritual forces the chance to re-create us, to make us over in a better mold. We open ourselves to receive guidance and to experience contact with the divine. Setting established routines to commune with Spirit is why monks chant Matins. It is why the ragas modulate the day.

For myself, a practice of three pages of morning writing is an effective meditation practice. At noon I walk my dogs, another break, and in late afternoon I bike-ride, an invaluable time.

"Dog walking! Bike riding! What does that have to do with spirituality?" one of my intellectual friends snorts derisively. He can understand my practice of Morning Pages—after all, those are *work*. What he can't understand is the notion of scheduled recreation being part of the spiritual path. He does not look squarely at that word: "re-creation."

Bombarded at all turns by the bad news of the world

we live in, it is easy to forget that for all its struggle, the world is yet shot through with the glory of God and the ever-present possibility of human kindness. It is easy to feel overpowered by world events. It is easy to forget that each of us has the power to make a substantial difference in our world.

EXPERIMENT:

You do not need to make your spirituality one more job that you must do perfectly. Your spirituality is inherent. You need only focus on it.

Structure builds the spiritual architecture of our day. You've explored spiritual practices. Now you must place them in your life. By establishing the cornerstone of spiritual structure, we build a foundation for productive, joyous days.

Experiment this week with building spiritual structure in your days. The following questions will help you to make that possible. Take pen in hand and explore your opportunities for spiritual structure:

1. Do you take "spirit time" upon awakening? How?
2. Do you, or could you, take a small midday break? Try one.

3. Do you make a place for spiritual centering at day's end? In what form? Music, writing, stretching out?

4. At what point in your day could you build a spiritual replenishment?

5. Have you considered using Gospel or Handel or Gregorian chant tapes in your car? As you do household chores? As you exercise? Try this.

HIGHER
COMPANIONS

~

"Maybe we could have lunch," I heard a woman's smoky voice say. I turned and saw an exquisite woman with snow-white hair, chiseled cheekbones, and glacial blue eyes. "I'm Julianna," she added, and extended a hand.

I agreed to that lunch, and it launched a friendship that spans two decades now. When it began, I was twenty-nine years old, fragile in my newly found sobriety and in the midst of a horrific Hollywood divorce. Julianna, a veteran of Hollywood and divorce, took me under a sheltering wing. An inspired actress and inspiring friend, Julianna became a spiritual companion, someone who helped me to find my own path and stay on it.

Those seeking a spiritual path often talk about the danger of "lower companions," those who can lure us into damaging and detrimental behaviors. What about the need for Higher Companions, those who can accompany us on our trek to higher altitudes, even lend us a hand and haul us up the mountain? When we falter on our climb, they stretch out a helping hand. Higher Companions are "believing mirrors." They reflect back to us an image of our highest potential. Sometimes we marry our spiritual companions. Sometimes they come to us as friends, as teachers or employers.

It is critical to creative and spiritual growth to seek out those who know how to nurture and encourage. Christ surrounded Himself with twelve apostles. He worked His miracles of manifestation in their believing midst. They reported to us the loaves and the fishes, the water into wine. Who knows? They may have egged Him on. "C'mon, Jesus, do something!"

In order to work our own miracles of manifestation, in order to bear the fruits of our spiritual beliefs, we *require* believing mirrors. Higher Companions are such mirrors. They faithfully reflect back to us our power and possibility. "Do it yourself," they say when someone lets us down. Or "I'll help you and we'll do it together."

"We helped each other" is perhaps the phrase that best defines Higher Companionship. That help may be a listening ear, a timely loan, a helping hand painting the back bedroom. It is support of the kind that says "Yes, you can, and I'll help you" rather than "Without me you can't."

Sometimes Higher Companions practice "tough love."

They say "You're drinking too much" or "This is the fiftieth 'perfect woman' you've run through. Focus on yourself."

Higher Companions tell us the bad news and celebrate the good news.

Higher Companions meet for breakfast and call long distance. They send the book and the note "Thinking of you" or the lovely embroidered cloth "For your altar" from Chinatown. They embody the kind of love Rilke described as "two solitudes that border and protect and salute each other."

E X E R C I S E :

You need not travel your spiritual journey alone. Pilgrims travel with fellow pilgrims.

Spiritual companions allow us to hit the bull's-eye of our values. When we find people who are for us believing mirrors, it's good to take the time to polish them a little. Spiritual companions are our booster rockets. They allow us to travel farther and higher. They boost our flagging energies and keep our trajectory true. Friends like these deserve special care and attention.

Draw a circle. Now draw a smaller circle inside the

first. Draw an even smaller circle inside that. Place the names of your friends in the circles appropriate to their spiritual value to you.

Your spiritual companions deserve acknowledgment for their importance in your life. Send them brief, appreciative notes specifically enumerating the gifts they bring to you.

Dear Julie,
No one listens with ears like yours . . .

Dear Sonia,
I appreciate your visionary optimism . . .

Dear Ed,
Your friendship is a cornerstone of my emotional security . . .

SPIRITUALLY

CORRECT

Like bad critics focused on the infractions of a constructed aesthetic theory, Spiritually Correct people focus on "rules," not beauty or content.

What I want to know is, how did all the rules get in here? Maybe they're so strict and skinny that they slipped in through the cracks like a tall, scary character that used to sit on my bed back in my drinking days. I called him the "vampire priest" because he looked kind of like the scary death guy from *Poltergeist II*. If you didn't see that movie, just picture an old skinny guy with sunken cheeks wearing coal black like he just slid down the chimney of sin.

That's what rulemakers look like. They are the thin-lipped, scary ones who haunt you if you aren't Spiritually Correct. They come in a feminine form, too, which

Catholics might know as Sister Very Nasty. I'm pretty sure all religions have them and, as I said, they sort of snuck into the House of God through the cracks and now they are patrolling the aisles like they own the place. They don't. God does, but they forgot that.

Spiritually Correct people aren't too long on honesty. From their perspective, honesty has bad spiritual grammar. You can't say "Stop it! I hate what you're doing!" in simple declarative sentences. No, you are supposed to use the tangled and tortured and Spiritually Correct form that goes "I am certain it's just me and something I should work on and an area where I need to do a little more work, but it really bothers me—and I know it's my problem—that you are standing on my *goddamn foot!*" But they leave out the "goddamn."

Spiritually Correct people think they are God's favorites. They think God loves them best because they are so *purrrfect*. So, they often act a little smug when they share the bad news that you are doing something Spiritually Incorrect and God might drop you for it. They love to say scary things like "I'm sure you couldn't be aware of this, but it's been found that eating chocolate can cause you to run away with Satan and burn in hell. There's a reason they call it devil's food!" Actually, they are usually a little more vague, like "I noticed you were eating chocolate. Are you sure that's a good idea? I mean, refined sugar can cause problems when you meditate. . . ."

Obviously, being so skinny and strict, they were not given the big gooey blobs of honey-soaked stuff you sometimes get handed after you visit the guru. They weren't told that an occasional hot fudge sundae might do a lot to improve their spiritual condition. They think if you *must* do something like that, you might want to try Rice Ice with Chocolate Fake on it.

Spiritually Correct people can be pretty exhausting and they sure make it hard to throw a dinner party. No matter how yummy whatever you cook may be, you can be pretty sure that somebody will disapprove of something. And say so in a Spiritually Correct Wet Blanket way:

"Oh, is that chocolate . . . ?"

"Mmm, I don't eat anything that had a mother . . ."

"I hope you don't mind, I brought my own little bag of Vita Greens."

Now, you might think that I am just talking about California here and pretending I am talking about everybody, but I've run into this in Upstate New York:

"What I think I need is a hamburger."

"A *ham*burger."

"Yeah."

"Don't you mean a veggie burger?"

"No."

"A turkey burger?"

"No."

I have never been able to figure out why it was more

Spiritually Correct to eat fish, but I'm a Pisces, so maybe I am just a little sensitive. . . . I have never been able to figure out why chickens and cows had different spiritual values. And am I the only one who hears the lettuce shriek when you yank it out of the ground? I will show you spiritual!

My theory is that it all matters. It's all sacred and we get further knowing that and holding it in mind than we do making rules about it. Personally, I think everything is conscious. Except maybe Spiritually Correct people who may be more like zombies.

EXERCISE:

You do not need to work to become spiritual. You *are* spiritual; you need only remember that fact. Spirit is within you. God is within you. You need only open an inner door to make contact.

Record your answers and share them with a good-humored friend.

1. Are you ever guilty of being spiritually correct rather than direct?
2. Are you vulnerable to being manipulated by people who are spiritually correct?

3. Are you able to admit to yourself those feelings that are considered spiritually incorrect?

4. Do you have friends with whom you can share spiritually incorrect feelings?

5. Do you vent your spiritually incorrect feelings to God, or try to keep them a secret?

YOU'RE TOO SMART
FOR ALL OF THAT
GOD STUFF

~~~

I once had a Beverly Hills psychiatrist tell me "Julia, you're too smart for all of that God stuff." I'm not really sure where this idea that God is for the intellectually impaired comes from. I do know that there's a creeping suspicion in some circles that God is for the gullible. As one bright woman phrased her skepticism, "You can pretty much believe whatever you want, can't you?"

Yes. But it does seem to me that a lot of the people who might be uncomfortable with the idea of God could do a lot better with the plain experience. In other words, experimenting with the possibility of God might actually be a fine place to kick things off. Sometimes I think we are so product-oriented in America that we approach God the same way we approach dating. "Am I going to marry this guy or not?" Maybe we should try treating God more like a suitor and less like an intellectual construct. Maybe we should take the easy-does-it approach and try going for a walk together or out to the movies. Maybe we should stop trying to "figure out the God idea" and instead just hang out a little. Movie director Martin Ritt once told me, "Cerebration is the enemy of art. You just do it." It seems to me that cerebration is also often the enemy of spirituality. Like art, we must "just do it." Too much cerebration gets in the way. It makes you dumb.

One of the things I've noticed about smart people is that they can be really dumb about God. Maybe it's because they get a little competitive and think that maybe they are God. Or maybe it's more jealousy, like they *wish* they were God. In any case, they seem to like to tear God apart and analyze God in the same way you might run down or talk about the most popular girl in class. For example, there are seven spiritual belts to aspire to, according to one book on how to know God.

Smart people have a million theories about God. And about a zillion more points to debate. They've got ideas about God that's right up there with listening to a bunch of gay men talk about Greta Garbo. And they say kind of the same sort of thing, "I know so-and-so once ran into . . ."

Actually, maybe God is like Greta Garbo to smart people. Always mysterious and wearing sunglasses around them. God's got a good sense of humor that way, I think.

A girlfriend of mine tells a story about listening to a bunch of very smart people debating the existence of God while a big fat harvest moon, ripe and gold, rose outside the window right behind them. That moon was God's little joke.

When smart people talk about God, they always remind me of film critics too. They haven't got a clue how to make the movie, but they sure get off on saying what's wrong with it.

For a long time I thought that if you wanted to know about God, you should read what everybody had ever said about God. Then it occurred to me, why not try to just meet God. When I did, the sunglasses came right off.

EXERCISE:

When we intellectualize God, we avoid metabolizing an experience of God. As we learn to *connect* body and spirit, we actually become more spiritual, not less.

Either dance for fifteen minutes and think about God, or answer these questions: (Actually, you could do both.)

1. Does your intellect ever interfere with your spiritual life?

2. What spiritual techniques have you learned to use to get out of your head and into your heart?
3. Have you learned not to indulge in spiritual argument?
4. Have you learned to slow down, enter the moment, and have a spiritual experience?
5. What gentle and soothing nonintellectual approach do you use to contact God—singing a hymn, reciting the Serenity Prayer . . .

EXPERIMENT:

Humility and humiliation are not the same thing. It is one of the great paradoxes of the spiritual life that voluntary reaching for humility elevates rather than lowers our spiritual altitude. In monasteries and ashrams, novices and devotees sweep, scrub, clean, chop, and cook. Doing so, they encounter their inherent dignity, that which is not dependent on job descriptions or outer trappings. Most of us have at least one area in our life where the grace to be a beginner would serve us.

Many an accomplished adult has found unexpected joy by going back to school to study a subject he or she is not accomplished in. Humility encourages receptivity. Higher forces speak to us when we are modest enough to listen. If idle hands are the devil's playground, busy hands are the angel's.

Undertake a simple, craftlike task. For example, scrub the kitchen floor. Clean the bathroom cabinets. Bake cookies. Sweep the garage. Fold the laundry. Vacuum your car. Dust your bookshelves. Polish your shoes. Do your mending. Simple, repetitive tasks move us from left brain to right brain. Problems dissolve and solutions emerge. Christ was a carpenter. He walked barefoot and heard the angels singing. Go for a walk in your most comfortable shoes. Walk slowly and listen to what the angels say.

TEACHERS

A young violist touches bow to string. Across the room, in a straight-backed chair, an older woman cocks her head to one side, narrowing her eyes. Sound fills the room. It is the first movement of a Bach cello suite. The movement begins in great tranquility, rises, and stirs to dramatic intensity. The young violist plays it start to finish, then rests her instrument across the front of her shirt.

"Now," begins the older woman, "what do we hear in the first three notes?"

Out of the tapestry of sound, she picks a few key threads, tugging at them sharply.

"Now try it again. And this time . . ."

When we think of having a spiritual teacher, we often think we must find that teacher in an ashram or monastery, that their vows must be made to an esoteric order. We imagine that our spiritual teachers must be religious. The truth is that great spiritual teachers walk many paths in life and learn the lessons they teach through many practices— few of them overtly spiritual. The great music teacher Joyce Robbins is lit by a spiritual radiance as surely as is a Buddhist monk. Decades in music have taught her "Beauty is truth, and truth is beauty." What she offers her young student is more than impeccable technique. It is impeccable honesty. "Here, precisely, is where you faltered. Here, where the note rang false . . ."

In my parents' hometown, Libertyville, Illinois, one of the great teachers was an elderly hairdresser named Libby. Libby's chair at the Sheridan Beauty Salon was as rich a source of spiritual solace as any confessional. A tiny woman with silvery-blue eyes and curls to match, Libby listened thoughtfully, then put in her pithy two cents' worth, often as wise a distillate as an Oriental koan. My mother went to Libby every Thursday for twenty-five years.

For me, my own father was a great teacher. Making his way in the world from age twelve, when he took a job driving an alcoholic salesman on his rounds, my father was a shrewd judge of people, but he used that discernment in innovative and positive ways. Yes, he could spot a con or a fraud in an instant, but he could also spot talented young people who lacked advantages just as he had. As he made his way higher and higher in the business world, my father carefully opened doors for talented young people of good character.

"I owe my whole career to your father," the president of an advertising agency told me. "He gave me a place to live for a full year and opened every door he could for me to help me make my way."

My father's generosity was quiet and personal. Even once he became wealthy his spending habits were modest. He invested quietly and conservatively, except in people. There, he chose his investments carefully and backed them to the hilt. Those he sponsored in turn sponsored others. None of this was done with any "show." My father believed in being low key but having high standards. He held himself to those standards and the rest of us learned from his example.

A great teacher is one who practices what he preaches—and may preach very little, if at all.

EXERCISE:

The universe itself is our great teacher. When we are open and teachable, we learn from many sources. Everyone's life abounds with teachers, and they come to us in many forms. Our great teachers may be our partners in marriage or in business. They may be our friends, our children, our bosses. People teach us both by their positive and negative examples. The national addiction to celebrity tabloids may be in part an addiction to vicarious learning—"I'd never do *that!*"

Take pen in hand and enumerate five teachers from your past, five teachers from your present, and five potential students whom you could teach. Extend yourself in gratitude to those who have taught you. Extend yourself in some form of service to someone you could teach.

These gestures should be small and concrete—a letter, a postcard, a lunch date.

PARENT BASHING

Late one balmy afternoon, I was invited to high tea in a palatial villa William Randolph Hearst might have envied. The assembled guests were spiritual seekers of all stripes—many of them discreetly Masoni. We sat at a table that cost more than Arnold Schwarzenegger's Hummer and was about the same size. No one at the table was under forty. Everyone was civilized and therapized. They had jobs, children, and a whopping cross to bear: their rotten parents. The dinner conversation was a litany of insensitivities and lack of attunement. I could practically feel the parental ghosts flocking around the ceiling, saying, "I did not!" and "Here's why I did that" and "I really, really tried." The more the grievances piled up, the more I wanted out of there. It wasn't because I was "in denial" or "being triggered." It was because I am pretty sick of Parent Bashing as a spiritual sport.

Parent Bashing reminds me of male bashing. There's truth to it, but it's not the whole truth. I remember sitting in the offices of *Ms.* magazine once and saying, "Let me get this straight. None of you ever had a nice brother or cousin or boyfriend or father?" That's how I feel about the way most therapists talk about their parents. I am pretty sure the reason that it's called "nuclear family" is that a lot of therapists seem to think that the parent-child bond is radioactive.

At the very root of most therapy is the assumption that we have been poorly parented, therefore wounded and rendered dysfunctional in our current relationships. So commonplace is this thinking that we seldom look at it squarely, realizing what an astounding assumption it is and how counterproductive and even destructive such an assertion may be to our identity. Therapy is a recent invention and, like modern furniture, it has its place, but that place has loomed too large.

It is a rare therapist who says "Now, let's focus on all the gifts and attributes you've gained from each of your parents and all your siblings." And yet, in "primitive" cultures, such honoring is assumed. "Family traits" are considered central to a person's identity. Family businesses ran through generations, but so did family gifts. Mozart came from a family of musicians. So did many composers. It was assumed that a creative gift might run through generations as surely as blue eyes or a prominent nose.

Therapized into discounting our families, we don't think "I've got Aunt Minnie's gift for piecrust" or "I've got Grandma Mimi's green thumb." Under therapeutic tutelage we trace the multigenerational roots of our addictive tendencies, but we fail to trace a love of words, a gift for photography, a flair for cooking. Positive traits are assumed to be personal. Negative traits are assumed to be familial. We routinely sever our roots except for major holidays and we find our families among our friends. In throwing away our family lineage, we render ourselves rootless and ruthless. If our parents are the source of our wounds but not our worth, we feel justified marginalizing them to an old people's facility we seldom visit.

In Asian homes, there is a very different perspective. Central to each household is an altar honoring "the ancestors." The beloved dead are thought to be a wellspring of wisdom and benefits. The concern felt is not for the damage done to us by family but by the possibility that we ourselves might shame or damage the family honor. The bedrock assumption is that the family has honor, intrinsic honor, that it has a gravity and worth from which we can derive our own.

Native American, African, and Aboriginal spiritual

streams all cherish ancestors. Until recently, we did as well. We are the fruit of the past. We are the seed of the future. We live, but life lives through us. As we embrace our elders, we become ourselves. Not only the blood, but also the dreams of our ancestors flow through us.

It is my sense that we are surrounded at all times by spiritual forces waiting to lend their support. They do not intrude, but they are instantly available. As an artist, I routinely ask for inspiration. It often comes with speed and specificity, along with the sense that it is not only as an artist that I should ask such help. Several months ago, I felt the persistent presence of my late mother. I found myself seeing my life through her eyes and with some alarm: How was it I'd never taught my daughter, her granddaughter, to cook properly? I began cooking lessons immediately. It is my personal spiritual experience that when we turn to our ancestors, we find they have been waiting for our approach.

When therapy replaced spirituality as the catalyst for change, it moved the focus for human growth from the heart to the head. It is, indeed, heady stuff to discount our family roots and see ourselves as "self-made." The real question is whether what we've made of ourselves isn't a nation of orphans, needy and self-centered, worried about our own futures because of the way we have mistreated the past.

EXERCISE:

Honoring our lineage honors ourselves. It deepens and strengthens our intuition. As an artist, I routinely look to the spirit of artists I have admired for clues as to how I, too, might succeed. My creative elders have taught me a great deal. Our personal elders can as well. As we contact our consciousness of our elders, we simultaneously contact the child part of ourselves that knew them. A practice of quietly sitting and directly asking guidance from our elders often produces surprisingly specific and creative new directions. Gather a selection of your family photographs. Take the time to label them, organize them into an album, and to select those that speak to you most strongly for framing.

The creation of an ancestors altar is an Asian tradition that would serve all of us very well. Your altar may be as simple as a windowsill, a bookshelf, a small side table. Select and frame the photos that speak to your heart. Add a candle and a small vase of flowers. Maintaining your ancestors altar, changing the candle, freshening the flowers, will routinely put you in touch with your personal family energies. You will find yourself cherishing and respecting the unique creative coloration given to you by your ancestral roots.

OPTIONAL EXERCISE:

Prepare and serve one familiar and beloved family recipe. You will both feed your positive memories and nourish yourself and friends.

GOD'S WILL

I am not sure where we get the idea that God's Will for us and our version of a happy ending are at opposite ends of the table. I don't know why we think that we might want to go to France, for example, while God might want us to stay home and wait tables at Joe's. Somewhere a lot of us seem to have gotten this idea that if something is fun, then it's not on God's menu for us. Kind of like "Okay, I want the lemon meringue, but God probably wants me to have the lettuce leaf, so I'll just order the lettuce leaf. . . ."

I think a lot of the ideas we have about God's Will are actually somebody else's bad idea, if not ours, then our culture's. We're still pretty sin-soaked and Calvinistic in some ways, like most of the great dancers were maybe forced to walk the plank while the *Mayflower* was crossing over.

Personally, I think God may love to cha-cha—and even

to slow-dance. I think God might have built in a sort of honing device that works like this: "Want to find Me? Look inside and see what makes you happy." In other words, dreams may not be cruelty from God but clues about finding the Hideout. Maybe a spiritual awakening doesn't mean "Okay, the fun's out of here." Maybe it means "Oh, the fun is beginning."

I think that maybe my dreams come from God and that my version of them is sort of the rough draft. I start to work on a dream and God comes along and finishes the sketch, or draws another doodle I like even better. I'm thinking about how to tolerate the goddamn lettuce leaf another time and God is baking the lemon meringue pie I really want or the coconut cream I like even better.

One of the problems with believing that God wants me on the lettuce-leaf diet is that then anytime I actually get a bite of something sweet, I am sure God is going to yank it away. This is what I call Indian-giver God. (Although why do we call it Indian giver? Weren't they the ones from whom things were always being taken away?) In any case, you get the idea. It's this belief that God hates square dancing and Dior and really gets off on Gregorian chant and burlap.

It has occurred to me over the years that maybe God's got a pretty full emotional keyboard and we are the ones who get stuck in the somber and depressing keys. We're the ones who say "Forget going to France. Be happy if you don't get the red-eye shift."

I am not saying that God's Will for us is always manic and cheerful like a Road Runner cartoon. I am saying that there might be a much wider picture than the part we focus on and a much nicer sound track than "Woe is me, here we go again."

When it comes to God's Will, I think we've got a tendency to act like God is one of the networks and we're in for another year of cop shows and yuppies who live in the same building. We have a tendency to expect God's programming to be "You live and it's not a lot of fun and then you die." We tend to get ideas that God is a very serious character—and that we lack character ourselves if we want God's Will to be anything other than the good shift at Joe's.

I have noticed that we have a pretty humorless version of God. We ignore baboons with bright red asses and hummingbirds and puffer fish and act like maybe the footage of war and famine is God's fault and God's Will and not our own nasty monkey business. If everything wrong, rotten, bad, and depressing is God's Will, then it really lets us off the hook. If famine is God's fault, don't send CARE packages. Let them thrive on the same lettuce leaf God wants us ordering at Joe's. If we're depressed and miserable—blaming it on God, the SOB, well then, it makes helping other people seem like one more dreary chore, doesn't it? Kind of like helping your sister clean up her room.

If, on the other hand, our idea of a good time might be all right with God, even something God might give us a hand with, well then, it isn't quite so hard to pitch in and help somebody else, is it?

It's my spiritual experience that if we remember the "play" part of "play nice," then God's Will doesn't seem quite so grim and scary. If we've got to wait tables at Joe's for a while, we might flirt with the cute Jamaican cook and learn to make Key lime pie.

EXERCISE:

Our dreams come from God, and God has the power to manifest them. Too often, we fear our dreams are "just our ego," and we hide our dreams from God. This cuts us off from recognizing and receiving spiritual support.

1. Do you have a dream you've kept secret from God? Collage this dream on poster board.
2. Do you have a dream you would pursue if you "just had more faith"? Write about this.
3. Can you take one action toward that dream?
4. Take that action.
5. What was the result? "Report in" on the page and to a carefully chosen, supportive friend.

EXERCISE:

One of our most persistent notions about God is the lingering fear that our will and God's will may be at opposite ends of the table. The truth is that God might be quite satisfied with the precise creature that we are, and God's will for us may simply be that we express our true values.

> *In the garden*
> *Every flower*
> *Has its purpose*
> *And its hour.*

We are intended to be what we are. We are intended to live and express our personal values. Take pen in hand and number from one to twenty-five. List twenty-five things you are proud of, not what you *should* be proud of. Set aside fifteen minutes and take pen in hand again. Explore what the list has shown you. Do you take an unexpected pride in physical accomplishments? In artistic ones? In your capacity for personal relationships? What values are expressed over and over? What value is expressed that you'd like to see more of?

Our values are as unique as our fingerprints. Do

you value beauty, adventure, kindness, consistency? Select one small action in accordance with your personal value system: Do it.

Make fudge for an aging aunt. Send movie money to a niece. Call an old friend. . . .

BAD JULIE

The first time I got in trouble for my theological views, I was eight years old and in second grade at St. Joseph's Grammar School. Our classroom was a tall, sunny room with very high windows—a pretty idyllic setting, unless you were listening to what was being taught.

"And so I am afraid, class, that your pets don't go to heaven, because they don't have the same kind of souls as we do, as humans."

No pets in heaven? This was disturbing news. There was Alice the dog to think of and Sheba the cat, not to mention Chico, the naughty little Hackney-Welsh pony. Without them, what would I do in heaven? Sit around and listen to people like Sister Very Nasty? I think that was her plan, because she was continuing with her version of events and it was really sinister, more sinister by the minute.

St. Joseph's Grammar School shared the village green with a small white church, the Church of Christ Scientist. Our church was big and glorious, red brick with vivid stained-glass windows. The poor little Christian Science church was very small and very plain without any stained glass or even any brick. It was made of plain, white boards, the kind that the wind could huff and puff and blow your house of worship down. Yes, I definitely felt sorry for Christian Scientists with their plain, no-frills religion. My best friend, Lynnie Lane, was a Christian Scientist, and when she went to church there were no fancy outfits like we Catholics had, no smoky incense, no Latin, no anything except talk and a few plain little songs. Yes, it seemed pretty depressing to be a Christian Scientist, and at first that's all I thought Sister Very Nasty was saying, but no. . . .

"And so, class, I'm afraid if any of you have any little Christian Scientist friends, you won't be seeing them in heaven either, because they are not baptized, so I am afraid they just aren't allowed. . . ."

No dogs, no cats, no ponies, and no Lynnie Lane? Sister Very Nasty was not talking about my idea of heaven. She was talking about my idea of hell. I shot my hand in the air, jumped to my feet, and told her so.

"Sister. You're wrong about God," I told her. "Of course animals have souls. Of course everybody can go to heaven. God is not mean!"

Sister Very Nasty sent me to the principal.

The second time I got in trouble for my theological views, I was attending a retreat at my high school, Carmel High School for Girls. The retreat master was a handsome red-haired priest named Father Morgan. He told us: "So, you see, heaven is like going to the movies with your mother and watching God on the silver screen."

We were teenage girls! Going to the movies with our mothers sounded not a bit like heaven, although it bore a startling resemblance to my idea of hell.

I shot my hand into the air, jumped to my feet, and told him so. "Father Morgan, heaven's not like that," I began.

Father Morgan sent me to the principal.

The third time I got into trouble for my theological views, I was a senior at Carmel and I was running for class president. "What this campaign needs," I thought, "is a little humor." I gave it some in the form of a large, brightly colored campaign poster that featured Christ rising from the dead, wearing a white toga and a campaign button that read "I like Julie." Under his bare feet, which were just gaining altitude, ran my nifty slogan: "Continue a proud tradition. Vote for J.C."

For this bit of merriment I was sent to a psychiatrist. Fortunately for me, she thought it was all pretty funny. Unfortunately for me, I did not learn my lesson.

The last time I got in trouble for my theological views, I wrote and directed a feature film called *God's Will*. "An ensemble comedy," the campaign poster read. But some people did not find it funny. God was an attractive red-haired lady golfer who liked to cha-cha and hit holes in one.

"That is not funny," some very serious (male) critics scolded me. I still treasure my *Variety* headline: " 'God's Will' Hit in Europe."

And so, I thought maybe this book should be called "Bad Julie's Spirituality Book." Because to some people, God is no laughing matter. Perhaps to God, neither are they.

EXERCISE:

We often mistakenly believe that high spirits and individuality are "not spiritual." The truth is, we are as individual as snowflakes—and that is perfectly alright with God, who made both us and snowflakes—although it is sometimes difficult for our human companions. This is another archaeology lesson. Answer in writing.

1. Have you ever gotten into trouble for your spiritual beliefs? You may wish to collage this experience.
2. Has your personal conscience ever differed sharply from what you were taught? Be specific.

3. Have you ever acted on your personal conscience rather than on your conditioning? Have you integrated this choice?

4. Does your concept of God accept you as you are? Name parts you wish accepted.

5. Has your concept of God shifted as you matured, or did you allow yourself to "outgrow" God rather than your old God concepts? List areas your new God could now support you in.

SNEAK

One of the things my spiritual life has made me is a sneak.
I routinely pray for guidance—and routinely get it—in the
form of firm inner directives that I call my "marching orders." "Move to New York" they might say, or "Call your
aunt Bernice." No sector of my life is immune to marching orders. The directives, if I ignore them, are repeated
with more insistence. Some people might call this guidance.
It is guidance, but it's also nagging, and this is the part about
being a sneak:

When I am spiritually badgered into taking some unlikely action, I have learned *not* to say "God told me to."
Most people think the "still, small voice" is a metaphor.

When I was married, my husband took a lively interest
in the usefulness of my guidance. He was nearly as gleeful

as I was at some of its accuracy, but he didn't like the fact that when I prayed, I experienced not a single pointed deity, comfortably anthropomorphic, but a sense of plurality, well-meaning *higher forces* whom I frequently made the mistake of referring to as "they." My "still, small voice" had a choral quality.

"What do you mean *they?*" my husband would ask. "They who?" I think he expected—or perhaps dreaded—the moment when I would reveal to him that my life was run by white-cloaked figures from a distant galaxy. We lived in Taos, New Mexico, where many New Age neighbors disclose just such sources of guidance.

"I never saw any white-cloaked counsel," I told my husband. "I don't *see* anything. I hear my guidance, and it feels more like a chorus than a conversation with God."

"Mmmm." This information made him uneasy.

To tell you the truth, it made *me* uneasy. I had been listening to "them" for as long as I could remember. When I consciously began working on my spiritual condition, the clarity and volume of my directives increased. So did the specificity. When I directed a feature film, "they" warned me about light leaks on some of the footage, and about the unreliability of my soundman. To my chagrin, they were right on both counts. I had heard, but ignored their warnings. My botched film was a great convincer. I listened with more frequency and open-mindedness. My marching orders evolved from mere directives into pages of spiritual overview, both planning and predicting my future with uncanny accuracy.

"Are you channeling?" my husband wanted to know.

"Just listening," I told him.

"Ask them about—" he would occasionally request. The information regarding his life proved useful and accurate as well. I became over time more and more reliant on this unsuspected inner resource and also more reluctant to talk about it. It was unpleasant to be met with aggressive enthusiasm and asked for predictions. I worried about "playing God." What if "they" gave me false information? But the information wasn't false. It was disturbingly accurate. They flashed me images of a friend's fibroid tumors. How could I not tell her what I saw? I began to feel sympathy for Cassandra, the ancient oracle revered and reviled for her prescience. Keeping my own counsel became increasingly prudent. I didn't want to be labeled a flake or an intruder. I didn't want to "play God." I began to zip the lip.

My inner directives sent to me to England to write a musical, an unlikely but highly successful venture. They told me my marriage would end abruptly with my husband's departure. It ended exactly as they said. They told me what work to do, what the reception of that work would be, and why I had to do certain pieces despite the difficulty of their reception. They seemed to hold a higher spiritual perspective than my ordinary waking consciousness. "Skywalk" I named it, as though I were getting a satellite view of my life. "Skywalk" could see something coming that on "Earthwalk" I could hardly predict. This created tension, if not actual difficulty. Obedience to my guidance, my "marching orders," could mean that I took erratic-looking, often preemptive moves.

"Why," my friends would ask me, "are you doing that?"

"Why not?" I learned to reply rather than go into my guidance. Its reliability, my own skepticism, my years of testing it, etc. It could be argued that I chose reticence over reinforcing my own doubts. I would, after all, do as the guidance suggested, and I might as well do it as painlessly as possible. And so, I became a sneak. I'm not alone in this.

EXERCISE

Often our spiritual experience and interests differ from what we consider to be "spiritually socially acceptable." Rather than take too much heat for our evolving interests and opinions, we may "go underground," exploring spiritual techniques and practices we find personally relevant but potentially controversial among our social set.

Take pen in hand. Do you have spiritual interests you conceal rather than reveal?

1. Are you sneaky about your spiritual life?
2. Do you secretly believe things you don't publicly admit?
3. Do you have any friends with whom you share your secret spiritual life? Can you take spiritual expeditions together?
4. Do you have any friends with whom you've learned not to share your secret spiritual life? What traits deter you? Remember them.
5. Do you know anyone who seems to have a spiritual secret, an undisclosed inner source of optimism and power?

IN A SPIRITUAL
KIND OF WAY

There's an awful lot of competition in the name of spirituality. I call it "My mantra's better than yours" or "My
guru can lick your guru." It's kind of the same thing we
used to get into about whether you bought a Chevy or a
Ford.

Now, I hate to be the one to tell you this (no, I don't),
but sooner or later all spiritual paths lead us pretty much to
the same playground. I call this all roads lead to Rome, I
mean om, I mean *home*. Sooner or later everybody seems to
figure out the playground rule: We're all in this together, so
play nice. It's just that "sooner or later" can take an awful
long time. And in the meantime we go through this ado-
lescent period where we're out to prove that our guru can
corner better: "Oh, yeah? Let me show you what Jesus
can do!"

And we get into spiritual wheelies. "I had the most amazing experience in meditation on Saturday. . . ." Or "I was holding the Scorpion for a really long time when I realized . . ." Or "I find that if I do the really high-grade wheat grass, my spiritual attunement is much brighter. . . ."

Of course, we don't say this is just bragging. We call it sharing. It's just that the kind of stuff we share is usually tinged by a faint whiff of "Aren't I special?" A lady once asked to interview me so she could determine if I'd ever had an "authentic" spiritual experience. I felt like she was asking me about my orgasms to see if they were the "right" kind, and I had pretty much the same instinct that maybe I wouldn't want to tell her about those and get graded either.

Now that we're on the subject, I would say that spiritual experiences actually *are* a lot like orgasms. Any kind is nice, and most of us manage some of them. Maybe it's just me, but when I hear people going on about the kind of spiritual oomph they are getting from their teacher, it sometimes does sound like they are bragging about how many times they climaxed. In a Spiritual Kind of Way, of course.

EXERCISE:

Many of us feel self-conscious about our spirituality, which can make us act awkward, stiff, even pretentious. We wear our spirituality like a mink coat—not so much for its serviceability as for its announcement of our stature. We need to be gentle and affectionate with ourselves as we explore and dismantle this all too human foible.

1. Are you sensitive to spiritual pretension? Find an image of snobbery in a magazine. Post it visibly.
2. Are you guilty of spiritual pretension? If yes, list five ways.
3. Are your friends spiritually pretentious? Explore this in writing. Confront "it," not them.
4. Have you learned to use humor to disarm spiritual pretension? Do you consider humor anti-spiritual? Write on this.
5. Do you recognize spiritual pretension as one more form of snobbery? You may wish to collage or sketch this answer.

BUDDHA PESTS

Out to dinner at a fine restaurant, as we were deciding between sparkling water or still, the normally sane woman across from me announced, "I'm reading about Buddhism, and so I'm trying to have no preferences. Give me either one. Isn't that spiritual?" she asked coyly. Bad Julie answered, "No. That's not spiritual. That's dumb. I'm an artist. I have preferences. This red, not that red. Art is about choices, and so, for that matter, is life." Several of the Buddhists at the table gave me stern looks of spiritual disappointment.

And so, I want to know why Buddha is laughing—or, at least, smiling so serenely—and Buddhists can be so serious. I look at all the jolly little Buddha icons and I think, "Did this guy really say that rule number one is Life is pain? It doesn't seem likely. It seems like the same kind of typo that usually happens when a spiritual leader gets translated into a religion.

Think about it. Maybe Buddha actually said "Life is gain," meaning that we all do better each time around, which I think we probably do. Maybe Buddha said "gain" and the little "g" looked like a "p" because whoever translated it was trying to do a yoga headstand at the same time. *That's* why it got turned upside down.

I don't know Buddha, but I do know he did his turn in the barrel with years of starving-himself-to-death asceticism. Maybe that's when he said "Life is pain," before he came to his senses and had a square meal and noticed that the thousand-petaled lotus smelled good and that the cobra didn't bite him after all. Maybe that's when he cheered up and somebody did his portrait.

That's my theory, but I'm afraid to tell it to any of my Buddhist friends because I'm pretty sure it would mean I am not spiritual.

I don't know about your Buddhist friends, but my Buddhist friends can be grumpy. Usually, I just lay it off to sleep deprivation from their getting up at five to sit zazen. I know that would make me pretty crabby. Sometimes, though, I wonder if crabby isn't part of Buddhism, or at least part of Buddhism 101. It seems to me that a lot of the time when people get into Buddhism they get into a blue funk at the same time. Or maybe they get into a blue funk and then they get into Buddhism. When they do, they meditate for hours and watch their minds like TV, which is what every-body else watches when they're depressed. I guess the difference is that in Buddhism you watch your own bad movie and in regular America you watch the networks. Either way, it seems to numb people out, although in Buddhism it's called "detachment."

I'll tell you what makes me nervous about detachment. It seems like sometimes people are trying to detach from the things they are supposed to be paying attention to. Their husband, wife, and kids, for example. "Child dies, leaf falls from the tree, same value" may be true in the long run, but that's a very long run indeed. I get pretty uneasy when people worry more about attachments than about their kids' homework assignments. I have this hunch that we can get so interested in our past lives that we miss the incarnation we're all sharing.

EXERCISE:

Spiritual solemnity may be an earmark of spiritual adolescence. As phases go, it's one that's nice to grow out of. We don't "have" to be solemn to be spiritual any more than we need to smoke cigarettes to be grown-up.

1. Are you guilty of spiritual solemnity? Find an image of your own solemnity.
2. Have you learned to laugh with God as well as fear God? List five spiritual jokes God has played on you for your own good.
3. Cite an occasion where you've seen God's sense of humor. Write a small dialogue between you and God about it.
4. Can you laugh about your spiritual shortcomings? If not, "confess this" to a friend.
5. Do you recognize your spiritual growth as well as your spiritual shortfalls? List five small steps you've taken for the better.

NEW AGE RAGE

If you've ever had an officially New Age person get mad at you, it can be a pretty scary experience. For one thing, New Age people don't believe in anger. (I guess they think it's God's mistake that we've got it.) It's a little too nasty and human. So, if you accidentally get one of them enraged, you activate their "I'm transcending this" tone. It's the tone other people use to say "I'm sure you don't know it, but you're standing on my foot." You see this tone with great 1940s character actors in comedy. What they say and what they mean are very different.

New Age Rage is usually disguised as quietly martyred acceptance. Then they say something spiritually correct, like "Well, I guess you need to do what you need to do and, of course, you do need to take care of number one, don't you?" Before you have time to think "Was that a little dig?"

they go on with the transcendence speech. "Of course we will all be thinking of you and we all wish you well and we all . . ." Meanwhile, you're thinking, "All I said was that I couldn't come to your party because I had a business obligation."

New Age Rage can get pretty down and dirty. "I'm sure you're really sure this is the right thing for you to do, because we would never want to have you act in any way that's not in accordance with your highest purpose." Up until then you may not have realized that the dinner party was about world peace, but you are beginning to understand that the fate of nations hinges on your showing up for dessert. That's when they say you must be turning them down to remain in your integrity. You're thinking how did your integrity enter the picture when it's on the sort of muzzled health threat. "Just take care of yourself. I'm sure we will see you someday. When you're less busy . . ."

By now you are reasonably sure that you've just caused Chernobyl. Or maybe only the *Valdez* oil spill. You've certainly done something pretty terrible, or else they wouldn't be using that dead calm voice other people use to say "Walk slowly forward and do not panic. There is a large cobra behind you."

EXERCISE:

Humor restores our perspective. Learning to see people as characters detoxifies our pain.

1. Have you ever been the victim of New Age Rage? Write this as a dialogue scene.
2. When someone's angry but pretending they aren't, can you allow yourself to know the truth? Choose one friend who validates your perception.
3. Are you able to say something direct when you encounter New Age Rage? Write what you would like to say about a specific incident.
4. Have you developed a technique to clear out the toxic aftereffects of other people's anger? Try a walk, a bath, a cooking spree.
5. Have you learned to use humor as a clearing technique? Try a comedy as an antidote to resentment.

REALITY

One of the things that really baffles me spiritually is this notion we've got that, spiritually speaking, the bad news is somehow more real than the good news. Did we learn this from CNN? Somewhere we got the skewed idea that if you looked at the world with spiritual eyes, you would notice that it was long on pain and suffering and short on joy and ecstasy. It was "Pollyanna" to notice the good stuff and "realistic" to notice the bad. Rodgers and Hammerstein were routinely criticized for their spiritual optimism about the human condition. Their uplifting message was popular and needed, but often attacked as corny, sentimental, and naive. This reminds me of how dreary and depressing dramas about lingering cancer deaths are Oscar material while great romantic comedies aren't.

I think that spiritually we often do what the news editors do when faced with something cheerful. "That's not a story!" we snap. "Let's go with the burning building and cries of agony." Now, I am not saying that the burning buildings and cries of agony aren't real. But I am saying that joy and beauty are just as real. We like to focus on the drama and leave out human-interest stories. The cozy and happy bits aren't hard-hitting enough to make our broadcasts. It reminds me of a trick the tabloids use. A movie star is walking up the aisle at an opening with an unknown escort and *snip!* out goes the unknown and the star is walking in all alone. We snip out the joy.

I have a friend I call Dismal Diane. She is a healer, but when you talk to her, she can sound like the walking wounded. The sound bites on my voice mail are usually about her exhaustion and her long-suffering piety in the face of impossible odds. Meanwhile, she lives on a happy little ranch with baby sheep and raspberry bushes and great snowy owls and red-tailed hawks and rascally raccoons. To hear the sound track, it's living hell. She may feel joy, but she sure won't mention it. She takes her spiritual calling very seriously, so her gears are either martyr or saint.

I have another friend who, when I mention dogs and flower gardens, snaps at me that I live in the "Martha Stewart school of spirituality." I think the line is pretty funny, and I haven't had the heart to tell him yet that Eden was a garden too. Just because you notice the roses doesn't mean you miss the serpent and the wriggly worms and the smelly shit they use for fertilizer. It just means you notice the roses.

In other words, it comes down to what do you focus on and why. If you edit out all the negative, you live in denial. If you edit out all of the joy, you also live in denial. If you present only your solemn and serious and dutiful sides, you are lying just as surely as if you present only the Bud Lite version of your life. Jackie Kennedy Onassis smoked like a fiend but demanded that any pictures of her smoking be squelched. She wanted to encourage a smoke-free Lady Jacqueline image. I think we could have handled reality. I think it's a much more habitable place than people like to let on.

EXERCISE:

A spiritual life is made of choices. Make self-nurturing ones. Mix introspection with outer action. First write, then take an action.

1. Name five things that are pleasant and enjoyable in your current life. Do one.
2. Name five things that are difficult and trying in your current life. Avoid one.

3. Name five people who are pleasant and enjoyable in your current life. Contact one.
4. Name five people who are difficult and trying in your current life. Avoid one.
5. Name five activities that make you feel centered, happy, and grounded. Choose one and do it.

SEX

God invented sex. Every bit of it. All the positions, even the fancy ones we think we've invented ourselves. God made the parts that fit together the way they do. All the ways they do.

God knew we'd like slow dancing. And dirty dancing. And African dancing and spinning like the Sufis do, so your underpants show. God wasn't embarrassed by any of it. I'm not saying God watched us like a porno film, but God was in on the whole thing, so to speak.

God invented making babies. God invented making whoopee. God invented tits and ass—and a few other movable feasts. What I'm wondering about is how we got so embarrassed about all of it? What I want to know was who decided God was a prude? And who got the idea that God would like us better if we gave up something so nice.

Isn't it a little like giving back a really great birthday present? (It is called a birthday suit, now that I think of it.) I wonder how God felt about the ones who handed it back and said "No, thank you." I know the theory is that that way they'll be closer to God, but did God actually want to get closer to them? I get sort of resentful when somebody refuses something nice that I've gotten them. I'm not saying God's like me or I'm like God—but we do have the same initials, J.C., and so maybe God wasn't too thrilled when we decided to say "Thanks, but take it back."

Maybe when we decided we should give up sex, we were actually giving up part of God. I think I might be on to something with this. Don't we have lots of stories of whores with hearts of gold? Maybe they were doing something right, not wrong. It's possible.

One of the things I've noticed is that getting laid does seem to cheer up a lot of people and make them nicer and a little less cranky. I'm not saying I'm great at sex—but I'm saying that great sex and sometimes even pretty blah sex can still make you think there's a God and you've just gone to heaven.

EXERCISE:

First, answer these questions in writing. Then, move out of your head into your body in Part Two.

I hesitate to say sexuality is our most ticklish spiritual area, but it is.

1. Do you divorce sexuality and spirituality?
2. Have you ever had a sexual experience where you noticed a spiritual component?
3. Do you associate sexual denial with virtue?
4. Do you think of your sexuality as being a spiritual gift?
5. Can you celebrate God through sexual expression?

Part Two:

The body is a wondrous spiritual receiving set. Many spiritual traditions know this and have devised intricate and intensive disciplines to intensify and clarify our reception of the body's spiritual information. Yoga, Tantric sex, vision quest, walkabout, African dancing—all of these use the body to open the door to spiritual perceptions. As should be clear, the door swings open both from asceticism and from pleasure. In other words, practices like fasting may get you there faster, but slower and gentler gets you there slowly, sweetly, and surely as well. So, be gentle with yourself. Be tender with yourself. Be physical with yourself in a form that delights you. You may want to:

1. Lie in the sun.
2. Get your hair conditioned at a salon.

3. Get a foot massage.

4. Walk on the beach.

5. Drive to the country and walk there.

6. Take an African dance class.

7. Get a massage.

8. Roast marshmallows and warm your toes by a fire.

9. Go for a bicycle ride.

10. Walk your dog.

11. Walk a friend's dog.

12. Buy new socks.

13. Take a scented bath.

14. Toss a football.

15. Collect five beautiful rocks.

16. Go on a roller coaster.

17. Go Rollerblading.

18. Take a beginning yoga class.

19. Go ballroom dancing.

20. Play a drum tape and move as it moves you.

Execute at least one of these ideas or one of your own in the same vein.

LINGERIE

⁓

One of my favorite films is *Black Narcissus*, a "spiritual" movie by the great Michael Powell. It features nuns living in a former brothel and a smoldering subtext between one beautiful nun and a handsome adventurer. Of course, the attraction is not consummated—oh, but it is there. Powell was on to something with this. Sexuality, spirituality, and sensuality are intermingled for me. I'm not alone in this. One of my girlfriends is a well-known spiritual healer. She recently underwent back surgery. I called to check on her progress.

"How are you doing?" I asked.

She confessed that she was miserable. There was a lot of pain.

I told her, "I'll send you my favorite spiritual antidote for pain."

"What's that?" she asked weakly, doubtlessly expecting a Bach flower remedy or perhaps an affirmative prayer.

"Red lingerie," I told her. "I don't think there's anything quite like it."

She laughed. "I'm with you on that one," she chuckled, "and to tell you the truth, I've discovered some exquisite, ridiculously expensive lingerie that fits me perfectly and I can order by phone. So, I've just spent a fortune. No doubt about it, good lingerie does more to improve my spirits than almost anything else I can think of." We both got off the phone laughing.

I don't know that a pair of marvelous, all-cotton boxer shorts would have the same impact for a man. But I do know that spirituality that includes a sexual and sensual element can go a long way toward mending up the chronic Western split between body and soul. Physicality and spirituality *are* inextricably mixed, just not in our culture.

How we misplaced this I'm not certain. Perhaps it fell off the boat as we crossed the Atlantic, pilgrimages having been a Christian tradition older than Canterbury itself. Unlike the Sufis, who saw swirling skirts as a gateway to God, our Puritan forebears knew the devil danced. (And some Fundamentalists know it still.)

It is routine in African and Native American culture to dance as a doorway into spiritual ecstasy. Aborigines pray on walkabout. Shamans plunge into the jungle on rigorous treks. Any veteran of the marathon will tell you that completing it is a spiritual experience. At the end of his long life, Joseph Campbell cited a moment in his youth when he was a runner as one of his peak spiritual experiences.

We have split apart body and soul, and then we wonder why we feel an absence of God. Certain He's not found in the body, that lowly temple, we forget Christ's incarnation as a man. We seek God in the realm of the Spirit, leaving our bodies behind. It is one of the great ignored or buried facts of our culture that God can be found through our physicality.

I was educated by the Sisters of Mercy, the Sisters of Charity, the Carmelite Fathers, and the Jesuits. This was heady stuff. So heady, it was disembodied. In those days, nuns and priests were swathed in great shapeless robes so that all you saw of their human form was a face. I remember our seventh-grade ship being rocked by waves of titillation when Sister Mary Carl confessed that as a girl she had been a championship diver. A nun! In a swimming suit! On a diving board! We were horrified and thrilled. A few years later, at Carmel for Girls, I remember joining my classmates on the sidelines of the basketball game and watching the young priests swoop and swish, a brawny arm suddenly emerging from the folds of a flowing habit to sink a hook shot. Sigh. In those days, it seemed that all priests were handsome, certainly Father David, Father Elliot, Father Finton, Father Brian, and Father Chester. The act of choosing a confessor had a sort of swoony intimacy.

Physicality and spirituality were continents apart, and there they were, inextricably mixed. I think they belong that way.

Bette Midler once remarked, "Give me the right shoes and I can play anything." I feel that same way about lingerie. As the wonderful old Vassarette ads used to proclaim, "Sometimes a woman needs a little unfair advantage." Lingerie, for me, is a festive spiritual joke. God and I both know I'm wearing something red.

EXERCISE:

Spirit expresses itself through our bodies. Body and soul are one sacred energy. Connect your body and your soul by treating your physical self to something nurturing. Buy one heavenly something. This is the moment of high self-worth. Go to Chinatown and buy bargain-priced silk pajamas. Visit Japan town for a soft cotton kimono. Go to Victoria's Secret (secretly, of course). Phone L.L. Bean and get a pair of cuddly flannel pajamas. Find something that embraces you like a lover and makes you feel beloved. It does not need to be expensive, but it does need to feel *expansive*.

BELIEVING

—◦—

Many of my favorite movies involve the intervention of otherworldly forces and beings in human affairs. The plots revolve around concepts like fate and destiny. The characters inhabit the afterlife as well as this one. A helping hand—or hands—often reaches through the veil. I myself recently wrote a musical, *The Medium at Large*. As all of this indicates, I believe in an intricate, interconnected, and supportive universe. I believe that our desires are prayers and that prayers are answered if we are willing to see their answers. I do not believe this because I am gullible.

The existence of higher forces friendly to our aims that work on our own behalf is absolutely central to the spiritual life of most cultures. Angelic beings flit through the pages of the Torah, the Bible, the Upanishads, and even through Buddhism. Believers outnumber nonbelievers on our planet, yet belief in spiritual support can be difficult to attain.

None of us trusts completely, perfectly, and always. All of us struggle with the dialectic between our skeptical and spiritual selves. Why else the prayer "Father, I believe, help me with my nonbelief"? Saints and mystics grappled with the dark night of the soul, that despairing season when they knew with certitude they had been abandoned. We forget that even the great believers suffer from disbelief. We shame ourselves when our own belief totters. We want to believe permanently, comfortably, and once and for all. I don't think it works that way.

Each of us chooses for ourself when to assign the presence of a higher hand to our interpretation of our worldly affairs. Applying to Harvard, Mark did not think to pray to St. Jude, the patron of impossible causes. Instead, he crafted his letters of application to the best of his human ability and only in cozy retrospect believes that his application received unseen spiritual sponsorship.

The shadows of doubt are part of the spiritual experience. They visit all of us. Priests, nuns, rabbis, metaphysical teachers, and channelers all confess to seasons of darkness in which they doubted the very message they carried. Believing, they disbelieved. Disbelieving, they yet believed. Even those with long spiritual experience at times found it difficult—even impossible—to trust the guidance that they prayed for and received.

The process of manifestation is what takes belief. Five years ago, my musical *Avalon* came to me as a spiritual slide show, complete and clear in every detail. Music and lyrics flooded in on me. Characters spoke, scenes unfolded, and all of it happened in such rapidity that I raced to keep up, staggered by the pace and by the sheer size and scope of what I was being asked to materialize. I saw the "what" of *Avalon* quite clearly. But the "how" sent me reeling. I wasn't a trained musician. How was I to bring in the melodies sounding in my head? I invented a system of notation; it worked well enough. But how was I to transfer my notation to music? How was I—how was I, how was I . . . ?

Like many another artist through the ages, I learned that the "how" came as needed, limping doggedly on the heels of the "what." The trick to finding the way lay in believing that a way existed. The belief itself seemed to create the path.

Ours is an interconnected world. We are the "web of life," as Native Americans phrase it. Thinking of ourselves not as isolated individuals but as parts of a larger whole, we lose our sense of astonishment when our particular needs appear to be heard. Perhaps they are.

Spiritual teacher Sonia Choquette suggests that doubters should keep a journal and record their "luck, coincidences, and synchronicities." Such journals are dangerous. They convince us that prayers may be answered. They convince us that we may be cared for after all.

"It's true that it happens"—that is an accurate encapsulation of my own experience.

EXPERIMENT:

Often we pray for guidance, help, and support, receive it, and discount it as coincidence. We practice a form of spiritual amnesia. We say we want a God who pays attention, but when attention seems to actually be shown, we shy away from calling that God. Spiritual teacher Machaelle Wright recommends that all of us write a spiritual autobiography, tracing the turning points where God or higher help may have nudged us in the right direction throughout our life. You may wish to undertake that task, but if it seems too daunting, you may want to try a miniature version first.

Go to the five and dime. Purchase a tiny spiral-bound notebook. Record any and all examples of synchronicity or possible guidance. Continue this practice for one full month.

SCHOOL

"Life is a school and we're here to work on ourselves," spiritual teachers often tell us. "It's all about lessons— lessons, lessons, lessons!" Did they learn this from the hapless Agnes Gooch in *Auntie Mame*, pregnant but chastised after her fling with a scoundrel?

If life is a school, I want a Montessori or a Waldorf school, where learning is the by-product of becoming interested and intrigued. Learning as a form of obedience has always brought out the rebel in me. It is just our luck to have a spiritual tradition involving a pettish God unduly interested in obedience: "I told you not to eat that apple!"

Based on the physical world, it appears to me we are involved with a creator far more interested in learning than in lessons. My garden neighborhood features an easy hundred specimens of roses—and not one of them stamped "lesson complete." Instead, garden by garden, rose by rose, God's intoxicating joy is revealed. How much more joyful and forgiving that perspective is!

"We're all born children. The trick is how to remain one," Picasso advised us. Clearly, the Great Creator retained a childlike glee in creation and re-creation. Each specimen of flora and fauna—the tiger lily, the ruby-throated hummingbird—has a glee inherent in its ecstatic design. What is a zebra or a giraffe but a gleeful artistic joke?

Joseph Campbell advised us to "follow our bliss" if we wanted meaningful lives but, stuck with the concept of a schoolteacher God, most of us feel that is not allowed. Call it our vestigial Puritanism, we are suspicious of the notion that spirituality may involve joy as much as duty.

A good friend of mine, Daniel, has just reinvented himself. After thirty years in Boulder, Colorado, he and his wife have moved to tiny Orcas Island off the Washington coast. His communiqués are filled with wonder. Grace has flapped into his life on large and awkward wings like the great heron a week ago or the huge eagle that lumbered into the air just above him early this morning.

"My wife is like a little girl, so happy that we've come *home*," he reports. "Home" is a tiny community where shops are filled with homemade pies, jams, and jellies. The island air is moist and soaked in the verdure of great trees.

"We are in the verdant void," my friend says happily, astounded at the nerve he and his cherished wife have just displayed. For the better part of a decade, they had felt displaced by Boulder's increasing commercialism. Life there was a lesson they were flunking—until they cocked their ears to the call of the wild that drew them west and north.

"We were called here," my friend says, his voice cracking with wonder.

All it took to follow that call was the willingness to abandon the notion of a schoolteacher God who had set for them in Boulder a difficult but compulsory course.

Life is not linear. There is no set curriculum that we ignore at our peril. We are faced less with lessons than with opportunities, choice points, tiny and large. Our need is to choose consciously, to be responsive as well as responsible, to be innovative and intrepid, to listen to the still, small voice that whispers "Go this way. This might work." Sometimes that voice eggs us on into terra incognita. We abandon the known curriculum and set sail in the direction of our dreams. This is a scary but exhilarating business. We learn from mystery as well as from mastery. If there is a "lesson," it is this one, articulated by André Gide: "One does not discover new lands without consenting to lose sight of the shore for a very long time."

EXERCISE:

Instead of focusing on our spiritual failings, let us first focus on our spiritual accomplishments. This is not vanity, this is an accurate assessment of our spiritual foundation. In Native American tradition, this is called "counting coup." This practice is personal and particular. Take pen in hand, number from one to twenty-five, and enumerate twenty-five actions you deem respectable. They need not seem respectable to others.

1. I stay in touch with my family.
2. I pay my bills.
3. I lie less than I used to.
4. I gave up smoking.
5. I volunteer in the literacy program.
6. I stack chairs and do cleanup at my 12-step meeting.
7. I recycle.
8. I neuter my pets.
9. I make homemade valentines.
10. I'm part of the parents' co-op.
11. I drive carpools.
12. I'm a good cook.
13. I keep the bathroom clean.

14. I walk my dogs daily.

15. I visit my father even though he doesn't recognize me.

16. I e-mail my children.

17. I pray for my friends.

18. I give clothes to Goodwill.

19. I tip well.

20. I pay fair wages.

21. I take family photos.

22. I *really* help with homework.

23. I do spiritual reading.

24. I go Christmas caroling.

25. I listen to my children carefully.

HUMOR

In India, saints have been known to turn exuberant cart-wheels, intoxicated by their love for God. They are said to be "God mad," and their antics are regarded with acceptance and perhaps a touch of envy. Exuberant excess in the name of God is a proud spiritual tradition—just not ours. The ecstatic mystical poems of Rumi and Kabir are drenched in spiritual sensuality. Spiritual ecstasy is an intoxicating state. Nothing short of being drunk on God will suffice.

By contrast, Western spirituality can be somber. Not for us great careening cartwheels across the lawn. No. For us, spirituality is a serious matter and, in many spiritual circles, humor is looked at askance. Humor, after all, is about anarchy, and anarchy wreaks havoc on control. Since much of our notion of what it is to be spiritual hinges on control, humor is the enemy. A lack of levity is a recognizable earmark of spiritual adolescence. The guru smiles and jokes. The tight-lipped disciples grimace at any break of protocol, any errant humanity. They are gatekeepers. The jolly guru is safely inside the gates.

Conspicuously missing from our predominantly Judeo-Christian spiritual heritage is the concept of the holy fool. To us, spirituality is dead serious. To Native Americans, by contrast, the trickster or clown was considered absolutely necessary to sacred occasions.

"Laughter chases the devil away," says spiritual teacher Sonia Choquette. That being the case, you would think we'd do more laughing in spiritual circles. When we do, the spiritual health is contagious.

When I was a schoolgirl at Carmel High School for Girls in Mundelein, Illinois, a great faculty favorite was Sister Mary Elizabeth, B.V.M. A short, stout woman with a genius in mathematics, she acted as an adviser in the NASA space program. This gave her a certain cachet with starstruck students. But our real fondness for her was grounded in the fact that she routinely carried a pigskin football through the halls and snapped spiraling passes at unsuspecting students, hooting with laughter when they botched a catch. It was Sister Benedicta who taught us theology, but it was Sister Elizabeth, with her high, good humor, who taught us the love of God.

Fifteen years ago, when I was struggling with single parenthood, I called my high school English teacher, Sister Julia Clare Greene, B.V.M., and asked for her prayers.

"I'm at my wit's end," I told her, "trying to juggle motherhood, teaching, and writing." She suggested I go see an old Jesuit priest who had counseled the spiritually troubled for forty years. I felt a little foolish; so many women were in my predicament. Shouldn't I be able to handle my problems? The old priest put me quickly at ease.

"We've all got problems and we all need help," he told me. I expected him to counsel me to pray, or perhaps to offer up my suffering. Instead, he reached into a desk drawer and pulled out a pack of what looked like baseball trading cards. He passed the cards across the desk. "These are my friends," he said. "Some people might call them saints."

Sure enough, amid the holy cards of conventional Catholic saints, there was a scattering of handmade cards, news clippings, or obituaries taped on stiff cardboard.

"When I'm in trouble, or need a favor, I call on my friends," the old priest chuckled. "Take the doctor there. When somebody's got a health problem, I take it to him. He owes me, so he hops right on it. Do you have any relatives who've passed over?" he wondered. I named a favorite aunt. "So, talk to her," he said. "She'd probably love to get involved." With a merry little laugh, he took back his cards and put them away. "It's always nice to have your friends around," he said.

Returning home from this counseling session, I found myself chuckling a little at my own seriousness. "He's right," I thought. "Spirituality shouldn't be so goddamn serious."

Years later, living in Taos, I went to see a medium—or, as he calls himself, a "medium large." Larry Lonergan is a tall, portly man with the vivid features of a 1940s character actor. Like that old Jesuit priest, he wears his spirituality lightly. "The first thing I need to tell you," he said, settling in to read for me, "is that there's some woman here with you. She claims she's your aunt."

"That would be Aunt Helen," I explained, and told him about the old priest and his trading cards.

"Exactly," Lonergan said. "They've got quite a sense of humor on the other side. We could use a little more of it here."

EXPERIMENT:

Dante called his masterwork *The Divine Comedy.* The popular joke runs: "Angels fly because they take themselves lightly." Laughter has proven to be, if not the best, a very good medicine.

Rent a divine comedy: *Splash, Topper, Big, Analyze This, The Muse, It Happened One Night, Bringing Up Baby, State of the Union, The Philadelphia Story* . . . the story of your choice.

If you'd rather read, treat yourself to a *Harry Potter* book. *That* is divine comedy.

THE SOUND TRACK

One of the things I have noticed about the movie of life is that the Sound Track is often what makes you scared or kind of cautiously optimistic. Remember in *Out of Africa* when they had that great expansive John Barry flying music? Well, just think if they'd climbed into that plane and started playing something-bad-is-about-to-happen music. We'd have had our hearts in our mouths. "Oh, my God, they are going to crash," we would have been thinking, even though they probably were going to land just as fine as they certainly did.

I've found it's very helpful to pay attention to what Sound Track you are playing. Let's say you get a great job opportunity. You can either play the creepy-monster-at-the-window-just-when-she's-happy-watch-out music, or you could play "Chariots of Fire" and believe it might work out fine.

Let's say you did meet somebody cute at the supermarket. You can either keep right on playing Billie Holiday or you can switch over to Doris Day. You can either stick with the sad, soft violins or go with something a little peppier and maybe Latin. You can either practice your cha-cha or make yourself crazy with hauling out "Wide My World, Narrow My Bed." It's up to you.

It's pretty hard to do mortal terror listening to "The Nutcracker Suite." It's pretty hard to do happy endings listening to Joni Mitchell's "Blue." It's pretty hard to avoid having a good time with Willie Nelson. It's pretty hard to avoid having a bad time with some of Bartok.

Some religions act like God listens only to classical. Some religions act like God needs gospel to wake up in the morning. Personally, I think He's got a soft spot for Tammy Wynette, and the Holy Ghost likes the Beatles. Needless to say, God lets us pick our own Sound Track and then just sort of hums along.

EXPERIMENT:

The music of the spheres can play in your living room.

1. Have you learned that you can literally improve
   the sound track of your life through playing music?

2. What is your personal safety music, the music that makes you feel comforted and spiritually connected?

3. What is your personal expansion music, the music that makes you feel exhilarated and spiritually expansive and exuberant?

4. Do you have a comforting phrase you can repeat to yourself as a positive sound track?

5. What negative phrase do you use to characterize yourself that you should eliminate entirely from your self-description? Write a positive affirmation and practice using it instead.

EXERCISE:

In order to flourish spiritually, we must learn to listen deeply—not only to ourselves but also to others. This week, take the time to listen for your own secret longings and make the time to listen deeply to someone else.

I have found that I often censor my own deep heart. In order to listen to it, I must ask questions that allow it to speak to me. Take pen in hand and imagine a conversation between you and your heart. You might ask it in the following questions:

1. What do you secretly wish?
2. What do you most enjoy my doing?
3. Who are your favorites among my friends?
4. Is there anything I could do to make you happier?
5. What are you worrying about?
6. Is there some little treat you would enjoy?
7. Is there anything you want to tell me?

Now phone a friend and arrange to meet for a heart-to-heart. Listen to your friend with the ears of your heart.

APPROPRIATELY
COMPLEX

You may have seen the ads. Two young women with moonstruck looks on their faces sit in the back of New York limo. The ad copy tells us that they are both in love with the same young man. The solution that it proffers is that they both take a stiff drink of something that is Appropriately Complex. Well, that's one solution.

For those of us who cannot cool out a little with a stiff drink, cooling out a little with God seems like a viable alternative. When situations feel complex and unworkable, they may, in fact, best be turned over to higher hands than our own. I call this vacating the poison playpen.

Just at the moment, three of my close women friends are engaged in what used to be called a catfight. I am trying to stay out of it, and the shrewdest way to do that is to write God a memo saying, "Take it. It's Yours."

I have found that sometimes when I step back and say "This is the poison playpen," I am led to other situations that feel less toxic, even enjoyable. When I insist on staying in there and "working this out" or "working this through," I end up getting all worked up and to no positive avail.

There *are* situations which do, in fact, feel too complex to be worked through by human means alone. Lives that have been shattered seemingly beyond repair are, in fact, repaired, often miraculously, with spiritual help. My close friend Mark shattered his life with a teen pregnancy and early marriage, finishing high school at night school. Now he himself is a Harvard-trained educator with five books to his credit, and the child of that marriage is in law school. Mark is nearly two decades on a spiritual path, and while he himself is a bright and capable man, he credits spiritual help with mending his life.

Lots of problems are appropriately complex enough to try God. Speaking for myself, I had to be cornered into trying that tactic. I got sober at age twenty-nine, after a decade as a hot young writer. Slammed into the wall by my addictions, I *had* to get sober, and getting sober was, well, sobering. I had an infant daughter to take care of, a mother dying of cancer, a nasty divorce to navigate, and then, of course, there was the problem I focused on: What about my brilliant career?

"Shelve it," I was advised. "Focus on your sobriety."

"But . . ." I protested.

"But nothing," I was told. "Without sobriety there'll be no career."

So, I cared for my daughter, cared about my mother, and tried not to care about sitting on the bench as a writer. As the months ticked by and my health steadied, so did my conviction that I would never work again. If God was taking care of my career, I wanted to fire Him and look for new representation.

"Trust," I was told.

And then my phone rang. It was my movie agent, sounding baffled. "I just got a call from NBC. They want you to write a TV movie on addiction."

"I'll do it," I told my agent.

"What I'm wondering," he replied, "is who submitted your scripts there?"

I decided the answer was too Appropriately Complex to go into it. What was I going to say, "God did it?" (God did it.)

EXERCISE:

I'm sure the answer's yes, that some of life is too complex. Explore your "yes" in writing.

1. Have you ever turned an appropriately complex situation over for spiritual help?
2. How did that work out?
3. Do you have such a situation in your life right now?
4. Why aren't you turning it over?
5. How can you turn it over to God? Is there a specific action you could take that would symbolize your letting go and letting God?

Try this: Buy, select, or make a God Jar—a container into which you place written prayers for guidance in troublesome situations. This is a specific and concrete form of "turning it over." It makes the act of surrender an active leap of faith.

DUNK IN THE
BARREL

One of the things that happens whenever you stand up for yourself spiritually is that you get to play a game I call Dunk in the Barrel. Let's say you point out that somebody in your church is a bully. It's true. You know it's true, but it's really scary to say so. But you say it. Christ did to the Pharisees.

That's when you get to play Dunk in the Barrel.

You might remember this game from traveling carnivals. Somebody sits on a plank above a tank of cold water and passersby lob baseballs at a target above their heads, and if they hit it, *splash!* There they go, into the barrel.

When you've just said the "emperor has no clothes" about something that's officially fine, you get to play Dunk in the Barrel big-time. Say what you think and even before anybody lobs a baseball you might just *fall* into the barrel. And being in the barrel is not fun; being in the barrel is swimming to keep your head above the Sea of Lies.

The Sea of Lies hits you with waves that say you were arrogant. That you were cruel. That you were "not spiritual." That everybody will hate you. That and waves of self-loathing. Now, the Sea of Lies is really only the amount of water in a tiny little barrel that you fell into or got tipped into, but it can feel like the Entire Ocean of Truth.

It's not.

EXERCISE:

This line of questioning may feel delicate. Pretend you're at your internist's and remember these questions are for your own good. Answer in writing.

1. Have you ever had a Dunk in the Barrel for saying something true but unpopular?
2. Who reached out to you with compassion?
3. Is anyone you know undergoing a Dunk in the Barrel right now?
4. What can you do to support them? Do it.
5. Have you learned to accept life's upheavals without punishing yourself for somehow causing them? Buy some great socks.
6. Have you tried using humor to gain perspective? Write an "un-poem" on your pain.

MY FUNNY
VALENTINE

Maybe it's because I was raised Catholic that I like to swear a lot. "Jesus!" I say if you catch me off guard. "Goddammit," I say when I do something stupid or feel particularly stumped by something—life, for example, or some Gordian knot of a relationship. Even this book—the goddamn spirituality book—came in for a few choice words. This can get me into trouble.

I remember teaching at a particularly highbrow spiritual center where they might have been expecting St. Julia. Somebody asked me a question, I stopped to think about it, and then said, "Jesus. I just don't know."

On the break a couple of worried women came up and asked me why I was so free and easy with taking the Lord's name in vain. Was I anti-Christian? They didn't hear me saying the same kind of stuff about Buddha.

"I just know Jesus better," I told them. "We've got the same initials and I'm pretty sure He doesn't mind."

"Oh." They went away, looking both relieved and worried.

I'm not worried. And I don't think Jesus is worried either. I think He was pretty good at communicating exactly how He felt. "Father, Father, why have You forsaken me?" He prayed, and although it's been explained to me a million times that He didn't mean it, that it's actually line one of an optimistic prayer, I think He meant it and it was His idea of straight talk.

Straight talk is my favorite kind of prayer. I know that we are often urged to use "great prayers"—and I know a lot of them—but that still strikes me as the Hallmark Card School of Spirituality. Pick the prayer that comes closest to what you mean and how you feel, or pick the prayer you aspire to and keep your sneaky little doubts to yourself. When I use a great saint's prayer, I get to visit that saint's attitude for a minute, but that can make me a little dizzy and disoriented and sometimes I do a lot better speaking from my actual spiritual height, which can sometimes be a spiritual midget.

"Help me with the goddamn book," I pray. Or "Tell me what the hell to do now."

So far, I have not been struck by lightning and I have not been locked out of heaven—although I may never teach at the Very Spiritual Center again.

MY FUNNY VALENTINE

My language swerves from bad to worse.
I need a God who lets me curse.
"Goddammit" I've been known to pray
When something doesn't go my way.
"God help me" is another prayer
When something happens that's unfair.
"Holy God, I need some help!"
That's another thing I yelp.
"Oh, dear God, I need you here!" is
Something else my God will hear.
I find that when I use God's name
He pays attention to my pain.

EXERCISE:

1. Do you beat yourself up about swearing?
2. Do you stick to rigid linguistic piety?
3. Do you use swearing for comic relief?
4. Do you swear to shock or to communicate? Both?
5. Do you have a God who speaks your language? If so, write that God a field report on how you are right now.

HEALTH

⌒

In the past two decades, we have witnessed an upsurgence of holistic health care in which physical well-being is seen as directly connected to our spiritual well-being. That's healthy. We have learned that positive thinking and the power of prayer can have a clinically verifiable impact on conditions such as cancer. That's healthy. We have learned that we can take proactive responsibility in our own healing. That's healthy too. Unfortunately, we have often interpreted this to mean that the inability to heal is due to a spiritual deficit. That's unhealthy. We routinely posit that anger, rage, and resentment cause cancer. It is a short hop from there to the judgment that illness in all forms indicates spiritual clay feet.

Romancing the Utopian idea of perfect health and physical immortality, we divorce ourselves from the human condition that encompasses sudden infant death syndrome, congenital heart defects, genetically carried neurological disorders, and the simple fact of sudden and untimely death. As we explore the biochemical impact of our spiritual condition, we are prone to fear-based distancing techniques that create an artificial barrier, an invisible protective shield between the sick and the well. Rather than embrace the immutable and humanizing fact that we are all dying at all times, we point the finger of scorn at those who die more quickly, wondering how they have brought it upon themselves.

We have books written with an authoritarian and derisive tone that sketch out the stages of healing and identify the spiritual blocks which are "why people don't heal." The deep and mysterious workings of fate, destiny, and karma are reduced to simplistic cause and effect. We have come full circle to a mechanistic view of the body. There is something terribly unhealthy in this view of health.

In our increasingly bionic times, focused on the artificial perfectibility of the human condition, we simultaneously open our lens to include the knowledge of ancient spiritual perceptions such as energy flows within the human body, and we reflexively close our hearts to the equally ancient gift of compassion.

Life is precious. Death is inevitable. We can ill afford to shame one another for our handling of either. Surely the soundest definition of health must encompass compassion.

It is not so simple as "those who can heal do." Although routinely maligned as mere mechanics with a mechanistic view of the body, Western physicians have long known the mysterious vagaries of healing to lie with forces beyond their surgical skills: The operation goes perfectly, but the patient dies; the surgery is botched, but the patient survives; life stubbornly lingers in some. The same fierce spark is swiftly snuffed out in others. Sometimes the dying live more fiercely and wisely than the rest of us.

For three years, my fierce but fragile father lived with an inoperable cancer in his lung. "Nothing can be done about it and I don't want to try," he told the family firmly. Not for him debilitating bouts of radiation and chemotherapy. Instead, he chose to design and build a house, knowing the odds were slim he would live to take occupancy. For many years my father had lived aboard a sailboat on a Florida key. Wrested home to the Midwest by his illness, he set his schooner-sized new home amid a sea of meadow grass beside a tiny pond.

The tiny house contained a proud cockpit, a high loft space looking out across meadow and marsh. Three days before my father's death, the family carried him from my sister's house to his own. Seventy-two hours later he would be gone, his departure as peaceful and sudden as a scarlet tanager taking flight.

EXERCISE:

Many of us experience less vibrancy than we wish. We do "enough" to feel "pretty good." Most of us know a few things that, when we do them, make us feel much, much better.

"Treating yourself like a precious object will make you strong." What could you do to strengthen your vitality? Health is more than physical. It is psychological and spiritual as well.

When my friend and long time collaborator, director John Newland, died, he was eighty-two years old, still planning and executing his work in theater. His death was a shock. He was so vital and full of life, abrim with ideas and enthusiasms. His widow, Areta, told me this: "Johnny was an optimist. To him, the glass was always half full."

All of us have the choice of perceiving our lives as half full or half empty. Optimism is a learned habit and a gentle discipline we can set for ourselves. We can learn to ask, as John did, "What next?"—to be self-starting rather than a victim of circumstance. We can learn to act our way into right thinking if we are pessimistic, rather than try to think our way into right action. Acceptance is often ballyhooed as the ideal spiritual attitude. People mistakenly accept the unacceptable. Often, what we are intended to accept is that we must act. When we do, we feel our conscious contact and an upsurgence of optimism.

Buy a sheet of posterboard. Arm yourself with Magic Markers. Draw a stick house that represents your life. It should contain the following rooms: family, friends, spirituality, physicality, creativity, work, entertainment, adventure, and service. List the qualities you want in each of these areas. Then list three small, concrete steps you *could* take to move toward your ideal. Allow your inner optimist to take some.

BEAUTY

As a young New York writer in my twenties, I remember
having a pitched argument with some young communist
atheists. They thought art was decadent and every bit as un-
necessary as God, who was comfortably "dead." As it turned
out, at least for me, neither God nor art was decadent *or*
dead. Both had simply been misplaced.

In medieval times, the cathedral dominated the consciousness and the architecture of the town at its feet. Composers composed and sculptors sculpted, all to the glory of
God. We conceived of angelic realms aiding and abetting
our own, and those realms were gloriously beautiful. As
well they might be, at the very gates of heaven. Humankind
looked with wonder on the natural world and saw it as
imbued with spiritual perfection, a mirror to the glory of

God. The exquisite order of the cosmos, resplendent in the stormy skies, the tides and seasons, were taken to be proof of divine order, larger and more luminous than the fretwork of human affairs. Music and mathematics were said to be the closest approximation of the spheres beyond our reach. Both were imbued with "elegance," recognized as a spiritual attribute.

Many of our modern lives are far removed from the natural world. Many of our modern lives are far removed from beauty and from elegance, and from the idea that beauty can be a mirror or a gateway to God.

Skyscrapers dominate our modern cities. The grandeur and glory of God is lost amid urban chaos and cacophony. Earthly beauty is often strewn with litter and marred by graffiti. When community life centered on the church, temple, or synagogue, it was a privilege to craft altar cloths, cultivate and gather fresh flowers, light tapering candles and incense. These aesthetic delights were considered to raise consciousness that we might better approach the Almighty.

It can be difficult to maintain a transcendent thought on the streets of our cities. "Curb your dog" can also curb your thoughts. We may hurry on our way, watching the inner movie, but we seldom turn the camera of consciousness onto beauty.

All of life, every scrap and morsel, is sacred, creative, and charged with meaning. There is beauty in a tiny embroidered handkerchief, beauty in the sweeping span of a bridge. There is beauty in what God has made and beauty in what man has made. And making beauty makes God manifest.

"The kingdom of heaven is among us," Christ taught. Blake believed that if the doors of perception were flung open, we would be dazzled by beauty everywhere. It is not reserved for museums or concert halls. It is in the kitchen and the clinic, the hospice and the hospital. Just as there is no subject that cannot be addressed by art, there is no aspect of living off limits to our creativity or to our own creator. The awakened eye sees art everywhere. The awakened ear hears music in the drip of a faucet, the scrape of a chair, the squeal of a brake. Holy, holy, holy, Catholics explain, bowing to the beauty of the Host raised on high. The mountains of Tibet, the thundering falls of Niagara, evoke the same startled shout of the soul, at once humbled and exalted. The exquisite statuary of the Orient exudes a powerful sense of the sacred even when yanked from its moorings and deposited in the sterile space of a museum. It is a circular proposition: The beautiful creates a sense of the sacred, the sacred demands we create the beautiful.

In our secular lives, we honor our rights of passage by dressing in clothing that heightens the occasion by its sheer beauty. An exquisite bridal gown, a first good suit for graduation, a special dress for sweet sixteen. These are the secular ways in which we carry the vestigial memory of beauty and the sacred being linked.

Beauty remains a gateway to God, although it has lost that label. To stand in a roomful of great paintings, to listen to a sublime orchestral movement, to walk the winding pathways of a botanical garden or stand in the multifaceted light of a stained glass window, is to feel the approach of a transcendent something—that we may no longer call God.

EXERCISE:

Just as an act of spiritual housecleaning can have an effect in our outer world, an act of physical housecleaning can have an effect on our inner world. When we enter a serene and orderly space, we often find our mood elevates and our sense of calm optimism increases. Turn an eye now to your physical surroundings. Take a moment to ask for spiritual guidance. Light a candle, a stick of incense, and take pen in hand.

1. List three small changes you could make in your work area.

   A) Get something to hold my paper clips.

   B) Frame a family photo.

   C) Get another small file cabinet.

2. List three changes you could make in your bathroom.

    A) Add low-light plants.

    B) Place a basket of seashells near the tub.

    C) Change the throw rug and add a tiny shelf to hold candles while you bathe.

3. List three changes you can make in your living room.

    A) Paint this room a wonderful welcoming color.

    B) Get the rug cleaned and clear the clutter out of the bookshelves.

    C) Find a better reading chair and make a genuinely enjoyable reading area.

4. Turn your attention to your bedroom now.

    A) Experiment with placing the bed differently.

    B) Add pillows so the bed truly feels cozy to you.

    C) Create a small altar on a bureau or bedside table.

5. Continue, room by room, change by change, to bring order, serenity, and simplicity to your surroundings.

While sometimes discounted as the "house beautiful" school of spirituality, experimentation with these
small changes will quickly register as a sense of
heightened spiritual well-being.

DISCERNMENT

One of my favorite images in film is the celestial records hall in heaven from Michael Powell's great movie *A Stairway to Heaven*. As souls step up to the reception desk, they are greeted by a serene, angelic maid who's got them right there on her checklist. Like Santa, she knows who's been naughty and who's been nice. We might call this "judgment" but I prefer the word "discernment."

Traditionally, we've had a sin-soaked, shame-based sense of spirituality. We were bad people trying to get good. Enter the New Age and the notion that we are all perfect exactly as we are and that to think otherwise is to be less than spiritual. This is where discernment goes out the window. Some of us are mean, some angry, some sarcastic, and we are intended to recognize this and act accordingly. Yes, in the long view we are all exquisite, all perfect, all imbued with God. That is the long view, and sometimes it is a very long view, indeed.

When we are told not to "judge," we hear this to mean we should not be discerning. This is not the case. Judgment involves condemnation. Discernment involves acceptance of often difficult realities. "That man is the cliff for me." Why not step back?

Compassion is the taproot of all flourishing, and sometimes compassion requires not only discernment but discretion. We must learn not only when to step forward in loving-kindness to others, but also when to step back in loving-kindness to ourselves. We are not intended to immolate ourselves on the altar of difficult people. Kindness begins to flow through our lives when we practice the great kindness of realism about where people are really at and if we have business interacting with them or not.

Often in trying to "improve" ourselves, we surround ourselves with difficult, contentious people, telling ourselves they hold lessons for us and that when we learn them, all rancor and difficulty will melt away. A) This is arrogant. B) This ignores free will. Our goodness may soften them eventually, but in the meanwhile we may have worn ourselves out, wasting years we could have spent with congenial companionship.

"Be nice," we tell ourselves when we begin to get realistic. Instead, we should give ourselves an Oscar for coming to our senses.

"Be positive!" we sometimes scold when what we should be positive about is that the situation is negative.

When we try to force ourselves to think good thoughts, we must take care to remain realistic. If Alfred is a nasty, mean-spirited man, our seeing that, accepting that, and moving on may be the best course. Each of us has free will. Alfred can and will behave exactly as he chooses. If he is angry by nature, our well-wishing may have an eventual impact, but discernment would suggest we steer clear.

Some of us pretend we are nicer than we are, but others of us routinely pretend that others are nicer than they are. Either of these positions throws us out of our own energetic grounding. The energies of others can be accurately discerned when we are willing to be honest with ourselves and stop pretending that our "goodness" can melt mountains.

EXERCISE:

We often think that it is not spiritual to practice the art of discernment. We think this, although Christ practiced it when he purged the temple of money changers. We think this, although Gandhi practiced it when he marched to the sea to protest an exorbitant and punitive tax law on salt. Discernment, which is frequently confused with judgment, is actually a faculty of wisdom.

The exercise that follows is a playful but profound game of discernment. Given to me by actress Julianna McCarthy, it is called "Whom would you take to the war?" You are asked to play this game, pen in hand, listing your family, friends, and acquaintances and why you would or wouldn't take them to the war. Some people are beloved but undependable. Other people are beloved but argumentative and would fight you on strategy. Others still are beloved but hotheaded. They would shoot before they saw the whites of their eyes. In light of this exercise, some friends step forward as superb comrades—shrewd, generous, dependable, and daring. Other friends fall firmly into that second tier—those whom discernment tells you you could not take to war. Life is not a war, but it is often a battle. This exercise helps to select your comrades in arms.

SPIRITUAL VAMPIRES

Much of the goal of dumbed-down, over-the-counter New Age thinking is to make ourselves impervious to the attitudes and actions of others. We ask for a wall of spiritual protection. We ask for energetic shields to deflect negativity. We try to use affirmative thinking to weatherproof ourselves against others' emotional storms. All of these techniques work. All have their place and we use them because some people are what I call Spiritual Vampires. They suck the life out of you with a big toothy smile.

Every person carries a distinct and personal energy. This energy and its resonance with our own is what we are talking about when we say "It's good to see Mary" or "Bob was really a drag." Embedded in our ordinary language is a kind of code that indicates our subtle energetic perceptions which we often make far more esoteric than they really are.

Reading Eastern spiritual literature, we encounter talk of subtle energies, but then we say "I could never feel that." But we do feel that. We feel it. We say it, and we often, at our own expense, ignore it.

One way to cast it simply is to recognize that each of us has both an adult component and a more vulnerable child-like component. In a balanced relationship with someone, both of these aspects are welcome. In an imbalanced relationship, one or the other will be welcome, but not both. When part of us is unwelcome, we will feel ourselves drained. We have met a Spiritual Vampire. . . .

Bob, a talented but embittered man, casts those around him into the role of rescuer. Gifted but unwilling to use his gifts, he wallows in a self-centered depression from which he longs to be rescued—but not by himself. Being around Bob is like being around a strong negative magnet. He wants to be a needy child. Anyone around him is cast as the caretaking adult. Selfish, self-centered, and intending to stay that way, Bob is high-maintenance and wonders why people intuitively avoid him. What he doesn't recognize is that he, too, would avoid himself, and that is exactly what he is doing by insisting that others meet his needs for him, needs he could very well meet himself.

Bob is a Spiritual Vampire. He looks like one and acts like one, but some vampires are disguised. Take Marilyn.

A beautiful woman in her mid-fifties, she has spent

decades caring for her power-driven, angry husband and their anxious, neurotic children. Unable to turn a tender heart toward herself, she finds it hard to turn a tender heart toward those she loves. Instead, she urges her children to "grow up" and act like she does, an automaton cut off from the feeling flow of life. Marilyn is fearful and judgmental of spontaneous people. At the office she is stern, humorless, and controlling—of course she is. She is terrified by the hysterical, childlike part of herself she has long ignored. Treating her ever-escalating inner panic like a stern, shrewish mother—"Shut up, I told you!"—she quickly dampens the childlike spirits of those around her lest any enthusiasm create a contagious effervescence and sweep her out of her carefully monitored role. Officially a caretaker, Marilyn is a Spiritual Vampire in disguise. Her energy is every bit as draining as Bob's. He drains everyone's adult side. She drains away everyone's childlike energies.

We are striving to reach balance. Those of us who are too adult must embrace our childlike energies and soften into play. Those of us who are too childlike must embrace our more adult selves and move into a sense of responsibility and power. We do not want to entertain—or be—Spiritual Vampires.

We are each powerful and delicate simultaneously, and that is what we must recognize when dealing with one another. If we move through life encased in only our own spiritual bubbles, we eventually become stagnant from our own self-absorption—self-absorption in the name of spirituality. If, on the other hand, we focus on the needs of others to the exclusion of our own, we become drained, depleted, and depressed.

Asked to identify our own energetic pattern, most of us intuitively know whether we are too self-absorbed or too other-oriented. It is a question of accurately assessing ourselves and coming into balance.

We can feel keenly, accurately, and immediately when people are open to our energy and when they are closed. We can tell immediately when someone wants only to take from our energy and not to engage in any reciprocity. We can get out the garlic and sink our teeth into that.

E X E R C I S E :

Don't be a sucker for spiritual vampires. Learning who drains our energy is an act of spiritual discernment. Take pen and sword in hand.

1. Have you ever met a spiritual vampire, someone who leaves you feeling mysteriously drained?

2. Have you learned to avoid the spiritual vampires among your acquaintances?

3. Are you able to recognize a spiritual vampire when you meet one?

4. What spiritual vampires have you successfully eliminated from your life?

5. Are there any remaining who should be shown the door?

SPIRITUAL
SEDUCTION

In the silent movie days, they used to call it "It," and if somebody had "It," you knew it—and make no mistake, usually so did they.

I was traveling in England with my friend, actor/director John Newland, who had sixty-five years of show business in his blood. We stopped in Glastonbury, a spiritual hot spot, where we met with a famous spiritual teacher in a tiny little dark pub. He entered like a rock star. The room seemed to light and glow. Was it his aura? I wondered. John leaned over and muttered, "He's certainly got a 'Big It.'" The phrase made it just a little harder to think we were all quite so spiritual.

Since then I have met a lot of spiritual people with a Big It. Maybe you have met a couple too. Rudolph Valentino, move over. I will give you soulful, meaningful looks and deep, burning eyes. I will give you smoky promises of union—with God, of course. They are just the stand-in, but they'll do in a pinch. Or a "spiritual" hug.

The Swoon Factor can get pretty high around some spiritual teachers. There is something pretty addicting about the Meaningful Glances and the Come Hither, Child embraces. I'm not saying it's sexual—all right, sometimes it is—more often it has more to do with Yearning. It's sort of a spiritual game of hard-to-get. You want me, you can't have me, God's got me, *Om Mani Padme Om* . . . which can sound an awful lot like na-na-na-na-na-na.

I'm not saying that the spiritual life is all smoke and mirrors, but I do think the boundaries get a little hazy. I do think the hottest thing about some fire walks is the teachers. And this is where I get into trouble; I think of some of these spiritual Svengalis as spiritual gigolos. I have watched a lot of good people get separated from their good money to support them. Energy is seductive and spiritual adulation is no exception. Maybe I lived too long in Hollywood, where there were a lot of Big Its, but to me the sexual slips of the gurus seem less shocking than they do inevitable.

Noble spiritual seekers have the same Ravish Me, Master willingness as a starlet with a star director. Lots of gurus have a sweet tooth and they've also got a candy store.

EXERCISE:

Spiritual seduction is like any other kind—there's a line out there somewhere that could snag almost any of us. Forgive but don't forget your own misadventures, pen in hand.

1. Have you ever been spiritually seduced?
2. Was it financially expensive?
3. Was it personally expensive?
4. What brought you to your senses?
5. Do you now recognize when you are being spiritually seduced?

SPIRITUAL WAIFS

This is a related little warning note for men.

I'd like to talk about my least favorite girl in class. I'll call her Winona, the Spiritual Waif. I should tell you at the beginning that Winona is a knockout, although you are not supposed to notice it. You are supposed to notice very large spiritual eyes and the way that she uses them, like big liquid pools for you to swim in. Winona might be blond or she might be brunette or she might even have red hair. I've met the full Clairol spectrum of Winonas, and I have come to recognize them the way you might watch for pretty little coral snakes in Florida. Isn't that sweet? you think— until it bites you and you die.

Just like those pretty little snakes, Winona talks in sort of a soft and wispy hiss and tells you how confused she is and how she's really too spiritual to figure things out in the big bad world and she could certainly use your help. Or maybe a little of your money. Although she doesn't like to use the *M* word.

Winona wants never to be crass. She wants always to be pretty cloudlike and vague and gently desperate, so that after she whines for a while in a spiritual sort of way, you tend to reach for your checkbook to fix things.

Winona would probably call herself something like an innocent little mouseburger. Don't you believe it. She's got a black belt in numerology and astrology and you can bet she sees you coming pretty much a mile away. For her, spirituality is a racket. If she can convince you she's too spiritual to live in the world, then you will have to do it for her. We used to call girls like this gold diggers.

EXERCISE:

Yes, it's time. This exercise asks you to name names. Clarity is *not* a lack of charity.

Answer in writing, *not* your financial blood.

1. Have you ever met a Spiritual Waif?
2. Have you ever been a Spiritual Waif?
3. Are you able to say no to spiritual manipulation?

4. Can you distinguish between enabling someone and helping him?

5. Do you feel guilty about your own abundance when faced with someone else's poverty? Conversely, do you feel guilty about your own poverty when faced with someone else's abundance?

THE FAME GAME

What confuses people about spiritual teachers is that they turn into celebrities. Of course they do. This is America and the Fame Game is one of America's favorites. Culturally, this is the game we know how to play and fiscally it's the game we get told to play. It works like this. You do something well. (Or not so well, but you've got good PR.) And you get famous for it and then you are a spiritual brand name and people want to make tiny little Deepak dolls, or maybe that's your own idea.

You get the same problems as any movie star: a mountain of fan mail saying "I love you. P.S. Could you do this for me?" and also you get invitations to get collected and be the in-house celebrity guru, all sorts of confusing things. You speak at power spots because you're so powerful. You get managers and agents and an entourage, because as far as

the Fame Game goes, there's not too much difference between being Deepak and being Leonardo DiCaprio. You
still get the wet panties crowd. Just the spiritual wet panties
crowd. So, you need people to keep things at arm's length
so you can walk to the limo and you also need to get a grip
on things yourself. Which isn't so easy with everybody
telling you you know so much about God, you might even
be God. Maybe you even begin to think so yourself. Certainly no human being in his right mind would fly city to
city, year in and year out, staying in hotel rooms, eating
room service, and lecturing on how to lead a spiritual life.
What's spiritual about being away from your family with
adult cable for company?

When you get famous as anything, but especially as
some kind of spiritual teacher, people project all kinds of
magic powers onto you. I am an artist who got accidentally
famous as a spiritual teacher. I once had a lady ask me if she
touched my skirt would she be able to write her novel. The
answer was "You might want to try writing." But people
don't always want to work. They kind of want what you
have but don't want to have to do what you did to get it. I
call this the Magic Wand School of Spiritual Development,
and some teachers do like to act like if they just wave their
magic wand over your life, you will get everything you
ever wanted.

Sometimes when I would go somewhere to teach, the
people putting it on liked to write what I call "Meet St.

Julia and walk on water" copy. It was like "Take this workshop and presto! Instant creativity forever!" I'd say, "Actually, you need to do a few things," but they hated that part. I sometimes thought people expected the creativity fire walk. Make no mistake: the spirituality circuit can sound like any other travelling circus—there's an awful lot of snake oil being sold.

Another thing that happens when you get famous is that the velocity picks up, and that, too, can be addictive and confusing. When you are in a different city every other minute meeting constant adulation, you might find it hard to make sane and grounded decisions. Spiritual celebrities, like any other kind, tend to act foolish under all the pressure. Velocity makes everything sound like a great idea for a while. "Oh, yes, faster, faster, bigger, better, whee!" Until you hit burnout, and then nothing sounds like a good idea even if it is, and then you start snapping people's heads off no matter how spiritual you are, because the truth is that you are still human after all and you're pretty goddamn exhausted. This is why spiritual teachers could end up trashing hotel rooms just like rock stars. And some of them do.

EXERCISE:

Fame is a spiritual drug. It is disorienting and addictive in ourselves and in others. And yet, our mythology around fame tells us it will solve everything. Share these answers with a good-humored friend.

1. Do you fantasize about being famous?
2. Do you believe fame will solve your personal insecurities?
3. Do you experience other people's fame as disorienting?
4. Have you ever had a little taste of fame and wanted more?
5. Do you realize there can never be "enough," since fame is a substitute for self-respect?

SLICK VELOCITY

⌒

You know the picture: the model, impossibly thin, impossibly chic, stares heroically into space, the saw-toothed Manhattan/San Francisco/Chicago/London skyline jutting aggressively over one perfect shoulder. Assertive, invincible, above all "hip," this model telegraphs to us the message that ideally we, too, are to be assertive, invincible, and hip. Armored by such a force field of personal superiority, who needs God? In the slick world of magazines we *are* God or, at the very least, fallen angels.

The magazine headlines, as well as the visual images, push the notion of invulnerability. We are told we can "empower" ourselves. We read about "sexual power," "the power of being thin," "the power of being fit," "the power of personal charisma." Nowhere in all this talk of "power" is the admission that sometimes we might feel a lack of power or a need to find a power greater than ourselves.

In the slick world, spirituality is either marginalized or sensationalized. We read of Hollywood stars and their gurus. We do not read about the very real spiritual needs of all of us. In the slick world, spirituality is as closeted as sexuality once was. Spirituality may be human, but it's certainly not hip.

In the slick world, models do not have aging parents or difficulty finding good daycare. They don't have a sister with an alcohol problem or a husband suffering bouts of extreme depression. Cellulite looms as a larger concern than higher consciousness. With their model lives, models don't need a God, but we do.

Needing a God, believing in God, turning to God rather than therapy, in times of crisis puts us in conflict with the world we are told we should want and the person we are told we should be.

Including God out, the slick world sends the message that if you're smart enough, with it enough, and "empowered" enough, God is a lot more dispensable than a Fendi handbag.

When celebrities admit to a spiritual practice, that practice is often dismissed as "so California, don't you think?" A star like Richard Gere might be a Buddhist, but media stories stress the strangeness of his spiritual path. It is made to seem a personal affectation as showy as his silvery hair. In the slick world, spirituality is a photo opportunity: "Deepak and Demi." Reduced to such terms, spirituality is cast as a fad, an embarrassing phase that some celebrities go through: the Beatles and the Maharishi; John Travolta and L. Ron Hubbard. As snappy as their prose, the writers' skeptical stance seeps through. "Get over it," their tone says.

The speed of modern life is an anesthetic. A rapid, adrenalized day blunts us to our finer feelings. More and more causes us to feel less and less. We become desensitized to others and ourselves.

We overwork and underplay. We work out until we have hardened our bodies and our hearts. We wear urban black the better to anchor ourselves in anonymity. We climb the ladder up into our heads, debating films, politics, and policies and with a passion we refuse to turn to our own lives.

Rushing through our lives, we become acclimatized and then addicted to velocity. We become entrained to a more and more rapid pulse. When anything or anyone threatens this numbing yet exhilarating velocity, we become angered. "Lead, follow, or get out of the way," we snarl. We lose patience with those slower-paced or slower-witted than ourselves. Life becomes about sharpness, cleverness, acuity, "the cutting edge." Ah, that is a telling phrase.

In our culture, most arbiters of the cutting edge are

those who have armored their hearts and climbed into the cockpit of their minds. Our magazines are devoted to fads and trends, the newest, the latest, the inside edge. We aim to be "caught up" and with what? Much of the fast-food reading in our culture is devoid of heart and steeped in quick-witted cynicism. The focus is on the veneer of life, on what is slick, shiny, and has dazzle.

I like to read the tabloids. We have a mythology in this country that tells us that more, better, faster, is always the answer, that fame is the panacea, that wealth is the cure-all. People like Tom Cruise and Steven Spielberg are perceived to be beyond human feelings, immune to gratuitous and savage press, laughing all the way to the bank, the possessors of perfect lives. The tabloids, exploitative as they are, nonetheless debunk the lie that anyone is immune to the human condition. We see glossy stars in their hair curlers caught at the deli on a bad day. We learn who tragically miscarried a longed-for child, who has an eating disorder just like our sister. In their lurid, peculiar neon prose, tabloids are grounding. They are the shadow side of the sleek press. They are the reminder that life is inescapable after all. And, too, they tell us the cost of velocity. It is a tabloid specialty to catch stars as they make their beleaguered way through customs, badly jet lagged, just like everybody else.

In California, there is a popular joke: "What did you have? A face-lift or a surrender?" The punch line is 12-Step jargon for the fact that when we surrender our incessant velocity, we look better. We feel better. And we *feel* better to others.

E X E R C I S E :

Speed is exhilarating, and it is numbing. At first we feel good, and then we feel less. Slowing down, by contrast, makes us feel more. First we feel worse. Then we feel better. Above all, we do feel. Collect ten magazines, a piece of posterboard, glue or a glue stick, some Magic Markers, glitter if you choose. Set aside an hour. Find a comfortable work area and pore through the magazines. Tear out any image that speaks to you of your life. Take the time to collect images of serenity, connection, abundance, adventure, cherishing, and any further images that speak to your heart, even if for no apparent reason.

Cue up a piece of beloved music. Select the images you will use to collage. Remember that you can use single words as headlines or exclamations. Enjoy. When you slow down and look at your values this way, what do you learn? Write about it.

NEW AGE HEALING

~⌒~

Recently, I attended a Beverly Hills dinner party where I was seated next to a distinguished physician. He had recently attended a creativity conference in Santa Fe, where to his evident disgust, he found that creativity was being discussed in such—to him—"nonscientific" terms as shamanic techniques and practices.

"It's all a fad," he told his amused fellow diners. For this man, his scientific schooling had rendered him open-minded enough to attend a creativity conference but not open-minded enough to look beyond his own paradigm. While he would be the first to admit that creativity involves brain waves, he would be the last to entertain the notion that shamanic practices like drumming, dancing, or walking might be natural ways of inducing the same altered states he would find acceptable if induced by biofeedback, to him a recognizable "scientific" tool.

Over the past twenty-five years, as the New Age movement has garnered both momentum and mockery, disgruntled scientists have begrudgingly opened the gates to such radical concepts as "prayer works" (Harvard)—acupuncture might work and yes, the ancient maps of energetic flows in the body can now be validated by modern devices.

And yet, for each tiny advance toward openness, there has been a predictable tidal surge of resistance. Some might call this healthy, even intellectually rigorous. My perception is that "threatened" might be a more accurate description.

Although our legal system is rooted in the concept of innocent until proven guilty, our intellectual courtrooms function in reverse: guilty until proven innocent. We consider this defense self-protecting. "Thank God for the F.D.A.!" Our system of checks and balances has recently been called into question. As AIDS and other activists have argued, we may need to be more open—and fast.

This is where our cultural parochialism trips us up. We stand on our short pedestal of several centuries of rationalist and dualist thinking, looking down our noses at other cultures' traditions and spiritual perceptions.

For a supposedly egalitarian democracy, we are, in fact, highly hierarchical. We have cultural and intellectual hierarchies that function like a series of gates. We are educated into specialization. At the pinnacle of our hierarchies we have experts who know more and more about less and less. We are ourselves the Johnny-come-latelies. We dismiss the shaman's use of herbs, roots, and berries, only to discover they are pharmaceutically accurate and sound.

We are terrified of opening the gates to our intellectual fortress lest the savages overrun us. Often we open a gate only to shut it again—fast!

I am thinking now of the recent explosion of interest in what is called energy medicine. No sooner did we open the gate to the idea that we might be able to heal intuitively through working with the body's energies in noninvasive, nonpharmaceutical ways than some of the very people who opened the gates began building a hierarchy of their own. Instead of being content to say "We can do this and learn more and more as we go," keeping the gate broad and gentle, there was, instead, a new arena for sharp-elbowed experts to compete in (and to cash in on by "certifying" others). We were told auras were "always" certain colors. Cancer and other imbalances would "always" (not typically) look a certain way, and if they didn't, you were wrong.

We opened the door to the notion—millennia old— that touch was healing, but then quickly added, "But don't let just anybody hang out a shingle as a healer." How much more interesting if we were able to stay less elitist, more stubbornly democratic, and gently, collectively experimental? We are so worried about practicing the healing arts incorrectly that we lose sight of the healing value of trying to practice them at all.

EXERCISE:

If the term New Age sounds a little dated, it may be because the New Age is here to stay. Ideas that a decade ago seemed far-fetched may now seem old hat. Practices that seemed radical and harebrained have moved into the mainstream. Meditation is part of the marketplace, and called "stress management." Acupuncture is covered by your HMO. Your pharmacy carries homeopathic medicines. You live in Kansas, but you take yoga. You live in Cambridge, Massachusetts, and you resist all of this with a passion.

New Age Quiz (respond in writing):

1. What is your reaction to the phrase New Age?
2. Does anything about the New Age put you off?
3. Does anything about the New Age intrigue you?
4. Do you engage in any New Age practices?
5. Are any of your friends involved in the New Age?
   To what effect?

If you have not yet encountered the New Age, you may wish to experiment:

1. Visit a metaphysical bookstore.
2. Send for a spirituality tape catalogue, *Renaissance Media* or *Sounds True.*
3. Listen to some New Age music.
4. Visit a New Age convention.
5. Experiment with *The Runes* by Ralph Blum.
6. Visit a metaphysical shop and examine their Tarot decks.
7. Experiment with aromatherapy.
8. Get a Tarot reading.
9. Consult a spiritual reader.
10. Explore a good New Age book like Shakti Gawain's *Creative Visualization* or Sonia Choquette's *The Psychic Pathway.*

12-STEP PROGRAMS

To the discomfort of both the spiritually traditional and the therapeutically oriented, we live in a time in which many people acquire their authentic spiritual paths through 12-Step programs. Can something free and leaderless be good for us?

A nonhierarchical grass-roots movement, 12-Step programs take on the flavor of their locale. In Manhattan, the patois of therapy bubbles through the rooms. In Los Angeles, the mechanics of New Age metaphysics inform and color perceptions. The "program," as members call it, is a vast and varied human version of the Internet. Shares are like starting up a search engine.

"I'm experiencing difficulty with my boss. He's a rageaholic. Does anyone have any experience?"

It is all a question of balance. Those who take too little

responsibility must learn to take more. Those who take too much must learn to take on less, to assign responsibility where it really belongs. Time spent in 12-Step rooms is a long, gentle tuning process. Groups function like a pod of whales. They listen and sound, establish a sense of their own spiritual position by how it resonates within the group.

The group's collective energy may ground or elevate the individual's. A terrible day at the office that left someone haggard and near hysteria gets grounded at an evening meeting into something smaller than Armageddon. Conversely, a nagging personal problem may get clarified. "That's it! My wife doesn't listen to me."

Much as the Internet has dispersed the centralized power of publishing, the 12-Step programs have dispersed the centralized power of traditional churches. In the 12-Step movement, all members are accorded spiritual equality and autonomy. No one's version of God is considered superior to anyone else's. There is no priest, minister, or rabbi to go through in establishing "conscious contact" with the Divine. Instead, the Big Book of Alcoholics Anonymous refers to this spiritual connection as "an unsuspected inner resource." In other words, no one need go through an operator. Everyone has a direct dial to God, however that God or spiritual source may be conceptualized.

12-Step work is spiritual work, not self-help, and yet, it

is currently modish to dismiss the 12-Step movement as "self-help addicts." Somehow, it is more politically correct to engage in the closed-system shared narcissism of a therapist-client relationship than the more open system of a group.

Part of this is our familiar preference for experts. We go to a therapist the way we go to the mechanic: "Fix it." We also pay for it—often through the nose—which can make us value it more highly. Make no mistake, some therapists are highly skilled and profoundly empathetic healers—but many are not. Many therapists, like the clients they treat, are caught in life from the neck up, intellectualizing and theorizing over problems and patterns rather than moving out of the comfort zone and into the messy slough of feelings.

12-Step groups are messier, but perhaps we ought to try viewing them as a natural offshoot of our stubborn American individualism. We are a culture of entrepreneurs stubbornly starting small businesses and learning the Internet at warp speed. Perhaps the proclivity for help-yourself help is a sign of our cultural independence, *not* our chronic dependencies. Maybe we are drawn to the spiritual autonomy of 12-Step groups out of the very American desire to "do it ourselves," the way we might build a mail order log cabin. It is possible, even probable, that the pundits have it exactly backwards—12-step groups may appeal to our inner anarchists, not our sheep. Maybe many "self-help addicts" are actually rather adventurous and exploratory spirits who enjoy the polyglot experience that 12-Step groups may provide. They may find it refreshing to mingle with people of diverse and divergent backgrounds. Far from appealing to the inner automaton, 12-Step groups may appeal to the inner anarchist, excited by the black market spirituality they encounter there.

12-STEP PROGRAMS

It can really take some bender
To make someone admit surrender.
No one wants to join the program
But addiction's like the pygmy's blowgun,
The poison dart that makes you think,
I think I'd rather swim than sink.

EXERCISE:

Anytime we have an active addiction, it stands squarely between us and God. Our consciousness is not focused on the conscious contact with a power greater than ourselves, it is focused on the access and availability of our drug of choice, whether it be alcohol, drugs, food, or a person. Carl Jung explained to Alcoholics Anonymous founder Bill Wilson that the most effective combat of an addiction was a spiritual approach. "Spiritus contra spiriti," Jung put it. 12-Step programs are not the only way to achieve freedom from addiction, but they are probably the most effective, most available, and least costly. Consider the following questions, pen in hand:

1. Do you have a relationship with any person, place, or thing that you consider addictive?
2. Do you think it is possible you may need to surrender this addiction and seek help?
3. What is your attitude toward 12-Step programs?
4. What are your emotional or intellectual reservations, if any, regarding 12-Step programs?

If you have an area in which you feel you *may* be out of control, or struggling with the issue of control, answer the following questions:

1. What incident or incidents have made you feel your life was unmanageable?
2. What behaviors have you done that contradict your own value system?
3. What percentage of your time is spent obsessing about "the problem"?
4. When did you first feel out of control?

5. What stratagems have you used to try to control your obsession or behavior?
6. What is the possible payoff for hanging on to this person or behavior?
7. Can you imagine a life free from this obsession?
8. Does this line of questioning make you very sad or very angry?
9. What do you think you should do about your situation?
10. When can you do it? Do it!

KINDNESS

~

For two weeks now I have been housebound, unable to venture away from the little gray-shingled cottage I call home. I sit writing on the gray velvet couch or venture to the wicker chair on the porch. I hate my confinement, but as confinements go, it is idyllic. I have a blush-pink rosebush in radiant bloom. My garden borders the horticultural splendor of my neighbor's garden, a magnet for butterflies, hummingbirds, and cats.

I hate being sick, I'm "never" sick—and being temporarily incapacitated fills me with rage, self-pity, and wonder at the great courage so many people display in far more challenging situations. I am not in a back cast. I do not have AIDS.

For the second time in my life, I have found myself

sensitive to electricity. It seems somehow connected to "bringing in" a large piece of work, especially music. When I am in fluorescent light, my body prickles, I grow dizzy and lightheaded, my joints ache, and I feel nauseated. I need to get out of it—and fast. Computers have a similar effect. Refrigerators are like flu. A regular electric light can cause my hands to tingle. I've been living by candlelight, searching for ways to ground this unpleasant and frightening response. I've read books on environmental illness, spoken to psychiatrists, psychologists, internists, medical intuitives. In one form or another, all agree that my vibration is too high and needs to be stepped down by any number of known means: diet, drugs, sound, physical exercise, spiritual practice. All of these modalities work. One or some of them will lessen my sensitivity sooner or later. My fear, of course, is that they won't, that my sensitivity will continue to spiral higher so that I end up like an ash or the mummy, something out of a science fiction movie, which is how the sensitivity can make me feel.

"Julia," I tell myself, "people lived by candlelight for centuries. Lighten up. Slow down. Surrender." Fat chance.

And so I sit with my lovely garden view, my two small dogs, and my craving to escape all this coziness, get in the car, and drive, drive to wide-open spaces and a less claustrophobic life. I am learning something, I suppose. It is the usual "lesson" of my own passionate, restless nature, a lesson I know by heart.

My near neighbor has an ailing heart. She is wraith-thin, pale, with large, frightened eyes. Two weeks from now she is scheduled for surgery, a prospect she faces by turning deeper and deeper into her Buddhist practice. Still, I can see her fear. She is so gentle, so fiercely alive, so kind. Kindness is what I am finding all around me through this illness. It is not what I expected. And yet, my gardening neighbor passes me the name of a yoga teacher and tells me she once passed through an anxious time that the teacher helped her to gently ground. I call the teacher, touched by the unexpected kindness and wondering at my own cynicism that kindness is unexpected.

At all times, in all places, good is present and active. In the midst of terror and suffering, goodness is still stubbornly afoot. People will be kind as surely as people will be cruel. We forget this. We are taught by our media to forget this, and when we remember it, our hearts ease. Kindness is possible everywhere.

For many of us, the great enemy of our kind impulses is our sense of time. We feel too harried and too hurried to take the extra little beat necessary to extend ourselves. And so, we notice the deli clerk's new hairstyle but don't take the second to remark on its appeal. We see the young mother struggling with a stroller, groceries, and a door, but we leave her to her business. We are busy with our own.

EXERCISE:

We speak of "the milk of human kindness" and "honey from the rock." Sometimes a little sweetness can go a long way toward improving our spiritual condition. Take pen in hand and list five things you could do to be kind to yourself and five things you could do to be kind to others. Remember to be specific and accurate about what *does* feel good, not what *should* feel good.

1. Get new shoelaces.
2. Buy a better hairbrush.
3. Get pretty stamps.
4. Buy the album you've been wanting.
5. Put lemon in your water and drink a lot more of it.

1. Send your sister racy red socks.
2. Send your daughter movie money.

3. Call your old teacher and inquire about her health.

4. Make homemade soup for a friend.

5. Send the Harry Potter books to your friend with the blues.

Now take one action from each of these categories. Be kind to you and to someone else.

RESTLESSNESS

I think we might have a blind spot going. When we speak of spiritual practices and the fruits they may bring to us, we are quick to mention "inner peace." When we picture the Buddha, we see him sitting, smiling serenely under the bodhi tree, fingers folded in a gentle mudra, worldly cares a thousand times removed. That is what we are after, an inner fortress of invincible serenity. We do not picture the Buddha in the long years after his enlightenment, an itinerant teacher with a mission. And yet, that is what he became. Peace may be one gift of spiritual practice, but restlessness may be another. Gurumaya globe-trots the world. Mother Teresa worked ceaselessly. Christ himself was a peripatetic teacher, ranging the Holy Land to carry his message.

Swami Muktananda came to America. So did Yogananda. If the lamp of enlightenment was lit in their own heart, they in turn became lamplighters for others. They taught by example and by word, and they taught ceaselessly. Centers were founded. Publications undertaken. There may have been the peace of dharma in all of this, but there was a great dose of restlessness as well.

The nun teaching the parish illiterate, the housewife gathering clothes for Goodwill, the eye surgeon donating his time and expertise twice yearly in South America— any of these is proof that an awakened heart may express itself by reaching outward, not inward.

Until his death at eighty-three, my friend Max Showalter led a lively spiritual life. An actor, composer, painter, and writer, he was active in community theater. His nativity musical *The Touch of the Child* was staged yearly. A hundred youngsters would come under Max's directorial eye. Like a lamp set in the window, Showalter cast an expansive circle of light.

"You can tune to the positive," Max explained. "In fact, you *must* tune to the positive. By doing that, you can experience higher realms. The positive is what we want to bring in. Spiritual realms are a reality, and people need to know that they are a reality. This is what I try to express in my work."

A shrewd, well-grounded man with a good head for business, Max was both worldly and wise. Far from considering his emphasis on the spiritual to be an avoidance of the business of life, it is instead a consciously chosen strategy for dealing with life.

Many think of the Dalai Lama as the pinnacle of human attainment. Despite the loss of his country, we see him as a man at peace. His may be the peace of right action, but action as much as peace is a cornerstone of his life. He writes. He publishes. He travels. He teaches. His is a searching intelligence and a peripatetic life. If this is peace, and it may be, this is an *active* peace. An awakened spiritual heart is often an activist's heart.

E X E R C I S E :

Sometimes we long to make huge, sweeping changes in our world. We want to make a difference but we don't see how we can. Big changes begin with small actions. "Which actions" begins with clarity. We must discover our values to know what actions will be valuable to us.

Make three vertical columns. In column one, list the persons whom you admire. In column two, list what it is you admire about them. In column three, list an action you yourself could take, inspired by their values.

Now answer the following questions:

1. What qualities did the persons you admire have in common?
2. What arenas of action did they share?
3. What did this teach you about your own value system?
4. What small personal commitment could you make in accordance with your values?
5. Make that commitment and act on it. Be certain you have chosen something small and doable. It is better to keep a small, regular commitment than botch an overly ambitious one and become discouraged.

SERVICE

St. Paul was blasted from his horse. St. Joan heard "voices," but for most of us service is not a clarion call. It is an inconvenient and unglamorous spiritual direction. And yet, responding to its urgings throws open a doorway in the heart, and through that open door destiny may enter.

A late autumn afternoon, a man in New Mexico slathers Turtle Wax on the flank of his four-wheel drive. Out for a drive, a neighborhood boy, the son of a divorced father two thousand miles away, spots the man and waves, "Hey! What were you doing?" The man signals, "Pull in." The lanky teenager unfolds himself from his old beater.

"First we'll wax mine, then we'll wax yours," the man offers.

For two hours, as the sun beats down, he patiently initiates the boy in the masculine ritual of car care. Just at dusk, as the light flares, the boy pulls out, his old beater shiny as enamel, his smile good-bye lopsided and huge.

"I just thought, show the kid how to do this," the man remembers. It was nothing dramatic, just a quick impulse toward goodness. The man and the boy have been friends ten years now. The boy has gone to college and his first job. The man's become a distinguished educator, his specialty, children of divorce. Who knows? The boy may have helped him equally. They both have showed each other toward the path.

A housewife in Akron, Ohio, hanging sheets on a line to spoil her family with their airy freshness, shakes out a swath of fabric and stops, dazzled, the cloth flapping in the breeze. "Everything is perfect," she has suddenly thought. Her love for her husband, their children, the sunny afternoon, the faint hiss of the Interstate a quarter mile away, all of it is *right*. She smooths the flapping sheet, anchors it with four wooden clips. So old-fashioned, why not use the dryer? Love, love hangs the sheet on the lines, so her husband's cheek can touch the freshness of the Indian summer breeze.

In the spiritual books, there are words for what has passed. Hanging out her washing, drenched suddenly in "oneness," the mother had a "unitive" experience. Prophets have them and mystics, and so do we. We're standing in the backyard or the driveway, not on Mount Sinai, but the impulse to serve our people suddenly opens the door to a sense of God, Good Orderly Direction, we might phrase it.

It is fleeting but real. The waves part or the clouds do, and there it is, the unseen form, "God's shoulder." We pray and our prayers are answered in passing. We need to be alert.

"How can I best serve you?" a former nun remembers praying. She was happy in her vocation, devoted to the grammar school children she taught. Two days later she received a call. A tragic car accident, Carol, the wife of Jimmy, her high school boyfriend—her one beau before the convent—had suddenly died. She'd left behind Jimmy and four children, all devastated by grief. The young nun called to offer her support. What could she do?

She spoke with the children. She spoke with Jimmy. She helped with funeral arrangements. She and another nun went back to the house afterward—dishes in the sink, laundry in the hallways. "He needs a wife, they need a mother," the young nun thought. Sheer as a cliff, she suddenly saw her future.

"Oh, my God! Oh, my God!"—at the kitchen sink, hands in the soapy water.

"What is it? Cut yourself?" her fellow sister asked her.

"No, no, it's just—"

How could she explain? She had said her prayers, asked for God's will, and now, hands plunged in dishwater, she knew what it was.

Carol had been her friend. Jimmy had been the one man she loved before she gave up men. Children were her vocation. Was she crazy? Would Jimmy ever want her? What of her superiors, her vows? And as for her, a celibate, consecrated, was this sudden rushing of her heart toward Jimmy love?

"How can I best serve You?" she had prayed. Dishes, laundry, casseroles, vacuuming, school clothes, schoolwork, weekend visits to keep the foundering ship on course. Jimmy's grief, her own, the children's. Thanksgiving, Christmas, bitter holidays she tried to help with. Prayers in her cell at night. The answer? Always the same: Jimmy and the children. Then she talked with her mother superior, cheeks burning, who thought she should talk with Jimmy, who spoke to her first, and then they went to the bishop and the Vatican, and all, miraculously, inexplicably agreed, this bride of Christ was now to be Jimmy's bride, that was God's will. Vows dispensed, new vows taken, the young nun became a wife. What, in God's name? "He needs a wife, they need a mother. How can I best serve You . . . ?" It had all become one.

One reason we believe prayers go unanswered is that we do not like the answers we receive. We are answered, oh, yes. We are guided, but what we hear is sometimes against our own plans, counter to our intentions.

We are asked to serve when our prayer may have been for the world to serve us.

EXERCISE:

When we hear the word "service" we often think of something we would *hate* doing. The best service is passing on our joy in something we *like* doing.

1. What do you do well that you could teach to another?
2. Is there some simple form of service you could undertake on a regular basis?
3. Have you noticed that service is a mood-altering drug that leaves you happy?
4. Is there a way for you to use your creativity as a form of service?
5. Does the word "service" make you nervous?

DETACHMENT

It is often remarked that one of the beneficial rewards of meditation is detachment. Detachment has an idyllic ring to it. We translate it: "Great. I won't get creamed anymore." We often equate detachment with numbing out, when its real meaning may be something closer to equanimity. We tend to think, "Detachment will mean I don't care anymore." In reality, detachment may mean something closer to "I care but I don't care that I care."

Often, we think of detachment as the magic ticket that will allow us to bypass the spills and chills of loving others. It may more accurately be the ticket that allows us to accept the spills and chills of loving.

In each day's march, we encounter events that loom large and may feel overwhelming. Yet, looking back a few months later, we find ourselves saying, "What was the big deal about that?" In other words, we have gained a more balanced perspective. This is what is really meant by detachment.

People tell me they want to detach, and I tell them that first they must *attach*. Spirituality is about connection to God and one another.

Pursued deeply enough, all spiritual paths lead back to connection. The renunciant abandons the world to discover God, only to discover the world *in* God and God in the world. The devotee who turns within to discover God within himself eventually discovers God within everyone. The Buddhist who relinquishes attachment to pursue enlightenment achieves in the end a tenderly awakened heart. "In the end" may take a while, however. As many people become as mired in self-centered spiritual practice as become snared in years of self-involved therapy.

It may be a mark of spiritual maturity to desire "connection" more than "detachment." When we are connected, we are fully conscious. We are both available to the present moment and to the overview. We can be present both for sorrow and for laughter. We no longer feel the need to distance ourselves from our experience. We enjoy equanimity. When we are connected, humor reenters the picture. We may be irritable, but we can laugh at our irritability. We find that we are detaching not so much from others as from ourselves. We experience a curious sense of equality. Our own plans and agendas no longer loom like a colossus over our emotional landscape. Often for the first time we experience ourselves as a worker among workers and as a friend among friends. It is a wonderful irony that in seeking to connect to the importance of all life we detach from self-importance regarding our own lives. We experience a great paradox of the human condition: We are all unique, all special, and all the same.

EXERCISE:

Very often we are too deeply mired in the events of our lives to attain an overview. Too often when we strive for objectivity we arrive at harshness. What is called for is a combination of perspective and compassion. We need to learn to accurately observe events as they unfold without listening to the rationalizing narrative offered by the characters involved. There is a wonderful creativity game that helps to make this possible. It is called "Watch the picture without the sound."

Choose a situation you have difficulty viewing clearly. Describe it in the third person, sticking to the facts of the situation so that you are, in essence, describing the action of the movie without the dialogue. It works like this:

The situation "I am a lonely, frustrated single mother, overtired and overworked" converts to "She is a single mother. She has two children. She has a full-time job. She spends her evenings with her children. She spends her days at work. At night she helps her children with their homework."

From even this thumbnail sketch, it is apparent that some support and some simple fun is in order. The feelings of being overwhelmed are no longer mysterious. In light of the facts, of course you are overwhelmed. In light of the facts, the necessary actions are obvious, although not necessarily easy.

GRIEF

I woke last night sometime after midnight. There was a high wind, the sound of rhythmic metallic slapping, and the strong smell of salt and air. For a moment, before I came to my waking consciousness, I was in the forward cabin of my father's sailboat. The rhythmic slapping was the sound of the closely tethered lines slapping against the mast. I reminded myself my father was asleep in the aft cabin just a few feet away. Then the wind howled again, more fiercely, and I was awake in my tiny blue bedroom, miles and years from my late father. I miss my dad.

To love is human, to care is human, to grieve is human. Each of us grieves at our own tempo, in our own way. There is no proper way to grieve. Some of us do it by storms of tears, some by mountains of work, some by paralyzing inertia. Some flail in it like a raging river. Some cross it like a trackless waste. It can be oceanic, heaving the bereft survivor like great waves that rise, then pass. It can be fine and subtle as the late autumn air, tinged with smoke and ashes. Grief is many things, but above all it is personal. It is normal. And no matter how we do it, we do not do it wrong.

Sometimes in "spiritual" circles, there is judgment concerning grief. There is a right way to grieve, a right time to grieve, a "spiritually" appropriate decorum for grief. This is nonsense, but it is pervasive and persuasive nonsense.

"Why can't I have more faith?" we demand of ourselves, as though grief were counter to faith.

"Why can't I see this as a beginning?" we badger ourselves, as though an ending weren't already a beginning.

"Maybe I should grieve longer," we will even say if new life rushes to the fore. Grief is intensely private, although we often do it in public. The depth of a person's grief, like the depth of a person's faith, cannot be measured by an outside observer. It is spiritual Nazism to demand that we goose-step our emotions into neat, orderly rows. The heart is unruly. The soul more so, answering only to God. An untidy grief can threaten those who cling to the rocks of spiritual certitude amid the turbulent flow of life.

Grief is tidal. It comes upon us and subsides. Grief is mysterious, sensual, and particular. The slap of a screen door echoes the slap of a sailboat's riggings. Time falls away. The wave of grief rises, then recedes. The moth-

chambered shell of experience is left in its wake. We are intended to grieve. Grief deepens the soul. Its timing and duration are God's business, not our own. Like the hand of a great storm, a great grief leaves us shaken but washed clean.

EXERCISE:

Grief is devastating, not only because of losing what we love, but additionally because of the loss of faith that may result. We lose not only a friend but also our sense of friendship with God. We're angered by God's action or God's timing. We're angry at ourselves for what was left undone or unsaid and we blame God for taking away our chance to say or do it. Spirit survives the death of the physical. Our relationships continue. We do have the necessary time to communicate what is in our heart. We communicate through our actions. Losing a beloved, we can:

1. Write a letter to the one we love.
2. Write a letter to God, venting our anger and asking for healing.
3. Create a personal altar to remind us to pray for our lost comrade.

4. We can "carry on" as they might have wished, extending ourselves in kindness to those they loved.

5. We can make a poem, a prayer, a painting, a song, a story, or a scholarship devoted to their memory.

6. We can make a gratitude list of all that they gave to us.

7. We can make a memory list of times spent together.

8. We can renew our commitment to a shared passion.

9. We can plant a tree in their name.

10. We can still talk to them. We can still listen for their response.

CHERISHING

Cherishing is a spiritual art. Because it is often grounded in creature comforts, we seldom recognize its celestial origins. There is something about a tiny pot of homemade jam that tells us that not only our friends, but God may love us too.

Cherishing says you took the time to stop, look, and listen to your friends. It means you remembered to buy a housewarming gift. It means a sick friend got a potted plant. It means a friend facing a tricky operation received a soothing CD. Cherishing is an act of willful rebellion against the frenzied tempo of the times. "You matter," the cherishing tells the recipient. To cherish a friend is to acknowledge that friend's dignity, to offer an act of witness in difficult times.

Elberta is the matriarch of a clan whose holdings include extensive real estate and a distinguished horse farm.
A widow, a grandmother, and the daughter of a Denver
metaphysician who tutored her in New Age principles long
before New Age was born, Elberta exemplifies cherishing.
Surrounded by apple trees amid manicured horse barns and
paddocks, she runs her considerable empire from her
kitchen table, where there is always a ready platter of cheese
and crackers, soda or coffee, for her stream of drop-by vis-
itors. Whether she is dealing with a migrant worker's wife,
the president of a corporation, the lawyer for her far-flung
holdings, or one of her granddaughters, Elberta's attention
is quick, compassionate, and gracious. Her spirituality is
grounded in accurate attention. She is discerning but not
judgmental.

"He's out to use you," she may advise a young woman
of her new suitor, but it is said without rancor, merely as a
warning statement of fact. Elberta's world is not without
evil or devoid of difficulty: a beloved husband lost to the
ravages of cancer, a promising foal who shatters a leg in a
freak fall, the alcoholism that erodes a longtime work relationship, debilitating divorce for a favorite friend. To Elberta, these realities are the challenges to be met with an
open heart. When pain enters her world, she neither denies
nor embraces it—pain, like joy, is allowed to circulate
through her heart. The key word is circulate. Prosperous

and prospering, Elberta sees no contradiction between the spiritual life and the material. Rather, she runs her material world along spiritual principles. Fair prices and fair play are the bedrock of her business practice.

Listening with an ear cocked to spiritual reality, Elberta picks up her cues. "Call Gladys"—a friend who lives in the Wisconsin farmland. "You haven't heard from her in a while." "Talk to Ralph about that load of hay from Colorado." "Get down to the kitchen early and start the chickens boiling for a pot of green chili stew." "Remember to check the rhubarb in the back garden, it might be time for pie." Operating effortlessly on an intuitive wavelength, Elberta picks up her cues for whom to pray for, who needs to be dropped a note, and what troubling business situation requires her focused attention.

"Look at that cat," she says to herself, drinking a cup of tea as her day winds down. A black cat on the adobe wall, the butterfly balanced on a fallen apple, the last rays of the fading light gilding the weather vane perched on the barn. It is all good. It is all noticed. It is all placed on the scales in her heart, where her savoring of life's riches counterbalances the payment of life's costs.

EXERCISE:

Cherishing is the act of concrete, loving, specific actions. It removes love from the arena of emotion and places it squarely in action, its proper home. Too often we cherish our beloveds in our heart but neglect to express our heartfelt tenderness. This exercise requires you to act on your affections. Choose and execute an action from the following list, or devise an equally festive and affirmative action of your own.

1. Send postcards to five friends.
2. Send pretty stamps to five friends.
3. Make cookies for your friends.
4. Buy a friend a bunch of good sage.
5. Make someone homemade chocolate pudding.
6. Buy a friend a jar of good honey.
7. Make a friend a special ceramic cup.
8. Send a friend your favorite incense.
9. Give a relative glorious bath salts.
10. Buy an orchid for someone you love.

SPIRITUALITY
SALESMEN

⌒

Maybe it's me. Maybe I can't just enjoy a good laugh. It's just that when some spirituality speakers talk—prosperity ministers especially—I find myself thinking of used car salesmen.

You know the kind of speaker I mean. The kind who winds up a crowd like one of those show-biz grande dames coming back for a "surprise" encore that they actually always do. You know, "I never do this anymore, but, oh, all right, here's 'New York, New York'..." And the crowd goes wild.

I'm probably just a spoilsport, but I resent getting wound up and emotionally manipulated in the name of spirituality. Somehow hearing someone say "God loves us and we're going to get rich, rich, rich!" makes me just a little uneasy. (Especially when they then pass the basket and say, "Act like you're rich!") I get the guilty feeling with the prosperity crowd that if I'm not prosperous enough, I might not be very spiritual. I might be thinking "small," the spiritual equivalent of having a little penis.

Maybe it's because I've spent some time around the movie business that I'm a little leery of what I think of as more-is-better "big dick" spirituality. Boffo box-office records marking spiritual high water leaves me a little queasy. It's a hop to "I'm rich so God loves me more." Once a woman married to a very rich man informed me: "I've just always had a great karma about money." She sounded like she was talking about having great breasts. Which she also had. The witch.

EXERCISE:

Many of us treat God a little like we treat the IRS. We have a lingering fear that sooner or later we're going to get a call. God's going to want to know the facts about us and money. He might even ask us a few questions like these. Tackle them on the page.

1. Have you ever felt manipulated in the name of spirituality?
2. Have you run across people who equate material abundance with spiritual well-being?

3. Do you equate material success with spiritual accomplishment?
4. Do you believe it is God's will for you to be poor?
5. Do you believe it is God's will for you to be wealthy?

Often we are afraid to surrender our lives to God for fear that if we do, everything and everyone will be taken from us. Eastern traditions speak of the dangers of "attachments," and, fearing that we will be asked to become renunciates, we cling to people and things as if they were our security. People fail us, things shatter and break, the only real fortress is God. But we fear being trapped there, alone with God, like Daniel and the lion.

There is an interesting and constructive exercise we can do to place our love of "things" in a new spiritual perspective. Very often we love something not for the thing itself but for the spiritual quality that the thing embodies for us. The fast car, for example, may embody our love of freedom. The exquisite vase may embody our love of beauty. Take pen in hand and create three vertical columns. In the first column, list the thing you are attached to. In the second column, list the spiritual qualities or attitudes that it symbolizes for you. In the third column, list an action or attitude you can take in order to embody that quality more directly. Things are often only a substitute for God. This same grid will work to help you free yourself from obsessive love of people. Very often the object of addictive love represents qualities we wish to—and can—attain for ourselves.

GOD AS WE
UNDERSTAND GOD

~⌐

"We all get the God we understand," actress Julianna McCarthy, three decades on a steep spiritual path, tells me. I can see that. My sister is a portrait painter, artful and meticulous. It would follow that her God is the same. That is God as she understands God, a God of small strokes, one building on the other, leading mysteriously and inexorably forward.

My friend Mark has faith in what he calls his "wheelchair God." Plagued by a bout of self-pity, he suddenly encounters someone whose sheer human courage in the face of terrible plight makes him believe in the invincibility of the divine spark within each of us. That is God as he understands God, a firefighter God, heroic, who plunges into a burning building to save us all. Mark's favorite hymn is "Amazing Grace." He believes in the miracle of lives transformed. He believes we can do that for and with each other.

My friend Francine is a several-decades Buddhist. Her God does not rush into burning buildings—or even notice them. In fact, her God would be unrecognizable as God to most people. Hers is a God so vast, so unknowable, and so far-reaching that to many, such a God would feel like emptiness, and yet, for Francine, this is the God that works.

Todd, by abrupt contrast, says, "I believe in a personal God and I always have." Not for Todd a vast, vague, and Buddhist sense of the Divine. His God is hands-on, as accessible as Todd makes himself available—which he does by a daily meditation practice. "It's nothing fancy. I just show up and make a contact."

"It's a partnership," an eighty-five-year-old nun tells me. "If all you do is pray for knowledge of God's will, you're letting God off too easily. I expect more from God and I get more from God. We are *involved* with each other. If I've got a problem, I pray about it. I take it to God expecting help, and I get it. Knowledge of God's will is just a starting place in terms of having an actual relationship with God."

For me, faith comes like the explosion of a flashbulb or a sudden lightning strike. Just for a moment I see the spiritual landscape, and my relationship to it makes sense. Without those flashes I stumble along in darkness, asking, "Is this where I am meant to be?"

A faith that works is a faith that works *for you.* Francine, the Buddhist, would consider the nun's God to be a meddler. The nun would find Francine's Buddhist God-beyond-God an unspeakably distant partner. As for myself, I get by with my lightning flashes, grateful to have vast swathes illuminated however briefly. After that, it's a long walk in believing darkness.

E X E R C I S E :

Many of us grew up with a disapproving-God concept. We believed in the concept of original sin that left us flawed and unworthy. In order to sense God's unconditional love, we must practice loving ourselves. Rather than enumerating our flaws, we need to enumerate and celebrate our virtues. Take pen in hand and list twenty-five things you like about yourself. Then answer these questions:

1. Do you believe in God "as told to you by . . . "?
2. Do you have a personal-God concept?
3. Writer Michael Graham calls his God "an artist, lover, and comedian." What would you call yours?
4. Does your God believe in you?
5. Do you believe in the God you say you believe in?

COMEDY VERSUS
TRAGEDY

I don't belong to the club that says this whole world is just an illusion that you manufacture with your mind. On the other hand, life does remind me of a movie, and I do think that we have a choice as to which kind we're going to go to see.

Lots of people seem to choose the Melodrama Movie. You can tell when you've got a Melodrama person on the phone, because if you ask them how they are, they tell you how their aunt is and how their carburetor is and how their health might be next year if they don't watch it. They never say "I'm okay, how are you?" They say "I'm okay, under the circumstances," and then they tell you, always tell you, the circumstances. In great detail if you let them. The people who have picked Melodrama from the playbill are tiptoeing along the edge of tragedy, from their perspective.

If you look carefully, however, it's more like farce. First this! Now this! Then that!

Sometimes I think Melodrama people are having a good time but don't want you to know about it. If they're in Las Vegas watching the dancing showgirls, they phone you and complain about the heat. If they are sneaking off to see the comic perform at midnight, you get the call that says they are doing it only because of their terrible insomnia, which forces them to come up with diversions. Melodrama people are a lot like silent film stars, they really know how to work it. They cue up the theme music and you can practically hear it tinkling along underneath as they talk. Their life sounds a lot like *The Perils of Pauline,* but they don't really want you to race over and untie the ropes. You are just supposed to think maybe you should.

Tragedy people are like the kind of date who wants to see only documentaries and art films about how awful life is. They keep a firm grip on the fact that people are dying terrible deaths somewhere and you should be thinking about that over dinner. When you are dealing with Tragedy people, they keep trying to draw your life to scale by saying "Okay, so you are upset about your job. At least you have a job." Or "Your eye is twitching in a funny way? Well, you can be sure your HMO won't cover it because . . ."

Tragedy people are the CNN crowd, and they can pretty much give you the down and dirty behind the scenes, really upsetting facts about anything cheerful you can think of. Tragedy people do not believe in happy endings, even if one parks in the driveway.

Then there is the Scary Movie crowd. They live pretty much on the cusp of catastrophe. If the Tragedy crowd likes to give you the grim details on nuclear seepage when you tell them you're going out to the desert for R&R, the Scary crowd likes to tell you about UFO abductions and serial killers along Route 66. If you talk to them very much, you start seeing the Monster at the Window out of the corner of your eye and somebody seems to have turned up the sound effects on sirens.

I am sure you know somebody from the Light Romantic Comedy crowd. That's the group who when you call to tell them you could use their help on Saturday moving things in the garage, they tell you about their date with Joe. If you tell them you just got a great job, they say, "Yes, but are you dating anybody?" This batch believes in meeting cute men at the supermarket, but if you catch them on a bad night, they may have snuck out to watch a weeper with the Melodrama crowd. When they're depressed, they watch *Now Voyager* instead of *It Happened One Night*. They think love is the answer, but they really mean romance.

One of the things I have noticed about God is that He lets us pick our own movie. And we're allowed to change genres whenever we want.

EXERCISE:

This inventory requires you to muster rueful humor.
Comedy *is* the best antidote to tragedy. Consider rent-
ing the great comedy *Soap Dish* for a "post task" detox.
Once again, a quick written inventory.

1. When you are depressed, what actions do you
   take? List five.
2. When you are depressed, who helps you to regain
   perspective? List three.
3. Are any of your friends addicted to tragedy?
   Name them.
4. Are you addicted to the tragedies of any of your
   tragedy-addicted friends? This causes time debting
   to yourself.
5. If you didn't take things so seriously, what might
   you risk trying? Name ten possible adventures.
   Take one.

ACCEPTANCE

Let me start with my trouble with Mary Murphy. She was this bouncy, bosomy blonde with big blue eyes and a peppy prose style. At the time we met I was this coke-thin redhead who wore hostility black and wrote for *Rolling Stone*. Mary wore pink and baby blue and wrote for *Esquire*. She seemed to have a small army of helpful men hovering around her in case she got writer's block and wanted to go out for a soda. I'd pretty much convinced men that I could get along fine without them and that writer's block was the name of my bunker where I kept the machine gun aimed at intruders. Do I need to tell you how jealous I was of Mary Murphy?

"Just accept it," I was told, possibly the worst piece of spiritual advice available without a prescription. I didn't need to accept Mary. I needed to see what, if anything, I could change. In me, not her. In other words, Mary was a clue that maybe I should let my hair go back to blond, retire the film noir wardrobe, and admit that what I really wanted was a little romantic comedy—something in short supply for *Rolling Stone* writers in those days.

Acceptance is often touted as the right move spiritually, and I think that an awful lot of us waste years trying to accept the things we are meant to change. Sometimes a hostile boss is not a chance for us to work on our patience and oversensitivity. Sometimes it's a chance to look for a new job. Sometimes our depression over a lack of meaningful friendships is not a cue to try to deepen our spiritual rapport with God. It's a cue to get out of the house and meet people. Very often, if I can't accept something with relative ease, it may be because I am not supposed to.

Where do we get the idea that acceptance is so spiritual? Where did we get the notion that spirituality was such an inside job that outward actions were somehow of dubious spiritual merit? We used to be told "Faith without works is dead" and "Move out on faith." Now we seem to be told "Take it up in meditation" or "Work on your acceptance."

Where did we get the idea that acceptance was like penicillin and that we should use it on every emotional virus we came down with? In my experience, if something remains unacceptable to me for very long, it is because it *is* unacceptable to me. Where did we get the idea that it was spiritually incorrect to find some things unacceptable?

Where did we get the idea that we should use spirituality to tune out the negative instead of to alter it?

Accepting the unacceptable creates resentment. Resentment creates rage. Rage turned inward creates depression, and depression is a great excuse for martyrdom.

"I'm working on my acceptance," we say with a long sigh, like we deserve a spiritual star, when what we really deserve is a whack on the butt and the urging to get back out on the playing field.

When we ask for acceptance and don't get it, it's not because God is hard of hearing. It's because the answer is no. We are not being told "Try harder." We are being told "Stop trying." We are being told "Move on."

Yes, there are situations where we cannot move on, but they are actually very few. There is almost always some action we can take that our pseudo-acceptance keeps us from trying. Our restlessness, irritability, and depression may be telling us to stop accepting the unacceptable and see what else is out there. Sometimes comparison shopping is a good spiritual idea.

EXERCISE:

Sometimes I feel the very topic of acceptance is unacceptable to me. (I guess I just have to accept that about myself.) I don't think any of us finds acceptance easy. These questions and tools may help.

1. Take pen in hand and list five situations you are having difficulty accepting.
2. List five reactions to those situations you are having difficulty accepting in yourself.
3. List one quality you don't care for in yourself but could accept.
4. Make up a humorous rhyme about that quality in yourself. For example:

My own tongue is like a razor
I'm glad I'm me and not my neighbor.

5. Choose a quality you find completely unacceptable in someone you love. Make up a humorous rhyme that allows you to laugh at the quality without shunning your friend. For example:

What I've got in common with Jim
Is we're both always thinking of him.

DOPE-DEALER GOD

Maybe it's because I am a sober alcoholic. (Okay, take out the "maybe.") I often think the glass is half empty, not half full. One of the things I fear about life is that I am going to run out of what I like and the liquor store is going to be closed and I am just going to have to shake it out, writhing and miserable, until the damn store opens again.

You can probably see how with that as a life view, I have had to work at savoring things. I know there are people who call this "practicing an attitude of gratitude." I just call it a really good idea for someone like me. And so, yes, I do count my blessings, and when that doesn't work I play show tunes. I have discovered that watching *That's Entertainment* is cheaper than calling my shrink. All I'm ever really after is a sense of renewed optimism, a sense that there might be enough after all or that the package store will open again some year. Usually, when I get into this kind of thing, it's because I am going through a bout of God as Dope Dealer.

When I am believing in a Dope-Dealer God, I believe that He has successfully gotten me hooked on something or somebody and is just about to take it away. You may have met this kind of thinking in a dark alley. It goes, "Wow, that was fun last night. I'll bet he never calls me again" or "Gee, I loved working with those people, but they'll probably never hire me again" or "I'll never find a Chinese silk shirt as nice as this one, so I'd better buy a hundred" . . . (before God takes away my supply).

I am not sure where I came up with the "beg and grovel for it" God concept, but I do know this is the kind of thinking that makes some religions tell you that you should give up ever wanting anything, so you can wriggle out of this scenario. I am not so sure that trying to deny my cravings or wriggle out of my cravings has ever worked for me. I do better admitting them. For one thing, I don't think God is fooled. I think that if I am praying only for God's will for me and the power to carry it out, but I am secretly hoping for another date with Fred, God knows it, so I might as well talk about Fred and admit I am obsessed and maybe ask for some help with the craving instead of trying to pretend I am not strung out so God the Dope Dealer won't know He's got me over a barrel and withhold the stuff or jack the price up.

"Okay, you can have Fred, but you'll never eat lunch in this town again."

So, I usually find that the best thing is to admit what's going on with me and ask for some help with believing that God's not a thug. I say things like "Help me focus on something festive besides kissing Fred." I say, "Great little finch, thanks for that." I say, "Now, about Fred again . . ."

When I try to ask God only what God wants for me, all my hopes and desires become dirty little secrets. Then I'm into a parent-child relationship with God, where I am like one of those awful kids who *acts* very nice when Mom is looking but is a terror behind her back. I do a lot better putting my cards on the table. Once I've done that, I am a little more able to listen if God's got some other plan.

EXERCISE:

Answer in writing.

Thinking of this exercise as cathartic and plan a movie or theater date to a divine comedy. The *go*.

1. Do you secretly think God is a thug?
2. When things start to go well, do you expect God to snatch away your joy?

3. When you get happy, do you get frightened?

4. Do you associate faith with hard times and not with good ones?

5. Do you secretly act as if God has a nasty character?

DEPRESSION

It is a quotidian New Age bromide to say things like "Pain is optional." I'm not so sure about that. It is fashionable to assume that pain, especially pain in the form of depression, means that you are doing something wrong. I'm not sure about that either. Physically, we speak about "growing pains," and spiritually, we have them as well. They are a normal, natural, and necessary part of the spiritual process. Depression is not, in my opinion, a malady that indicates the immediate need for medication, nor, for that matter, meditation. Depression is a signal, and it can sometimes be the signal that you are doing something right, perhaps integrating a large personal loss at a deeper level. Perhaps recognizing an ignored intellectual hunger that asks you to seek new horizons. None of us likes depression, and the drug companies know this. While medication for chronic, unremitting depression may at times be appropriate, the acceptance of occasional depression as part of the human condition is also appropriate.

Depression is an interesting animal. It is a shape shifter. We no sooner identify it as depression than it breaks apart and shifts shape into anger and grief. We can learn like matadors to provoke depression into revealing the conditions that caused it. But depression is nonlinear. Things bother us that "shouldn't." We need to sleuth our way through recent events and personal exchanges to track down the culprit.

Adele's ex-husband remarried. She found herself engulfed in depression. "I was outraged by my response. What was I doing? I wondered. I didn't want him and she did. What did I care if he was with someone else? My husband was a high-maintenance diva. He sucked the energy out of everyone around him. I should be *glad* he remarried." But Adele wasn't glad, she was depressed. And judging her depression didn't help. Instead, she walked the beach and mourned the loss of her long-term marriage at a deeper level.

One of the seldom mentioned keys to the spiritual life is acceptance. Not acceptance of others but of ourselves. So often we focus on what we want to change, how we want to work on ourselves, lessen our character defects. Implicit in all of this is the unspoken idea that somehow God has made an error and you are deeply flawed exactly as you are.

What if there is no error? What if our flaws are foibles and not fault lines? What if we are acceptable even in the times we have difficulty accepting ourselves? It is the nature of the desert to be a hostile and forbidding place. Yet, within all that, there is a sheer beauty that emerges from the barren landscape. The same hard-won gains come from enduring the desert of the heart.

It is at least possible that hard times come upon us not as punishments but as stringent blessings. The poet Theodore Roethke, himself a depressive, tells us: "In a dark time, the eye begins to see." Spiritual and creative breakthroughs are the frequent fruit of time in the desert, a sudden vivid flowering as when the desert floor comes vibrantly alive after a rare and sudden rain. Droughts can be survived. Desert time can be turned to good purpose if we are willing to listen and endure.

EXERCISE:

The seasons of the heart are mysterious but to a purpose. Often when we feel the most barren and devoid of hope for no apparent reason, something is germinating deep inside us. All spiritual traditions teach that time in the desert brings with it a new vision. Desert time may precede a substantial shift in life direction. It may be the winter prior to the sudden, abundant blossoming of a creative spring. Knowing this can make it easier to bear—but not much. Here are a few gentle guidelines for desert time.

1. Continue your spiritual practice no matter how fruitless it feels.
2. Pray despite your resistance to prayer. Consider it an experiment in open-mindedness.
3. Walk. Get outside and get outside yourself. Remember St. Augustine's advice: "It is solved by walking."
4. Allow yourself silence.
5. Mend something broken.
6. Light candles. They are good company.
7. Get bodywork.
8. Drink far more water than usual.
9. Pay attention to your dreams.
10. Keep a journal in which you work the following phrases:

If it weren't so crazy, I'd say . . .
If it weren't so silly, I'd let myself . . .
If it weren't so risky, I'd try . . .
If I didn't have to do it perfectly, I'd allow myself . . .
If it weren't too late, I'd . . .

If I had enough money, I'd . . .
If I had more time, I'd . . .
If it weren't so nuts, I'd . . .
I wish I could . . .
I wish that . . .
I'd like to try . . .
I'm getting interested in . . .
It could be fun to . . .
The reason I'm in this spot might be . . .
I think I'd enjoy . . .

It is part of spiritual tradition to offer sweets to those in the desert. You could:

Make a fruit salad.
Buy a jar of good honey.
Slice an apple and cook it with water, butter,
and a little cinnamon.
Buy some hard candies.
Get bag of oranges.
Treat yourself . . .

Above all, treat yourself like a precious object. It will make you strong.

CLEANING

~⌒

We grow up learning that "cleanliness is next to godliness," but it's easy to hear that clause as meaning "Oh, wash up," or even get a notion of British colonial superiority, comfortably secure, gazing at the messy pagan thatched huts and believing in a Christian God made manifest in gleaming flatware.

Oddly, the experience of cleaning something often opens a direct channel to spiritual experience. Scrubbing the floor seems to scrub clean the window to spiritual vision. Convents and monasteries have long assigned their novices the tasks of sweeping and scrubbing. Perhaps there is some higher wisdom afoot than the lowest on the pecking order have to clean up.

In his poem *Pippa Passes,* Robert Browning correctly observes: "God is in His heaven / All's right with the world." Although we seldom make this connection, it *is* easier to find God if all is right with our world.

Cleanliness is serene. Order is grounding. Chaos is confusing and emotionally harrowing. Many artists report that it is in the act of ordering their desk or studio that they suddenly sense a right direction for their work.

Creative angels may be talking to us all the time, but cleaning something up may quiet us down long enough to listen. Spiritual teacher Sonia Choquette advises her students that clutter distracts them from their intuition.

"How are you going to learn the finer vibrations of what you're thinking if you have a million messy details distracting you?" she asks. And so, although her students think "Sonia's crazy," she sends them home to sort and toss. Inevitably, they come back to her with spiritual breakthroughs.

Sorting and tossing is a profound spiritual practice. We handle item after item, saying, "This is important to me" and "This no longer is." As we do so, our values swim into view.

Remember, humility opens the door to the heart. Remember, it connects us to ourselves, and it connects us to God—the God within. Remember, when we turn quietly to a small task, we ourselves become the good shepherd, soothing and quieting our restless hearts. It is a paradox that when we turn to the small, we successfully connect to the sense of something larger than ourselves that is benevolent.

As we gently and creatively cherish our lives, we develop the skills and insights necessary to living. Scrubbing the kitchen floor, polishing our beloved old boots, mending the torn pajamas, repotting the stunted plant—in any of these small endeavors we connect to God in the form of Good Orderly Direction. Insights flow into us as we garden or chop vegetables for a pot of soup. As we husband the life we do have, we are guided properly in the direction of the life we wish to have. Inspiration comes in the form of clarity—and often what comes clear is a small something, which leads to a small something else, which in turn leads to a large change in direction.

My sister, Elizabeth, a portrait painter, lives on a horse farm. Her tack room features an old, glowing Oriental rug. It looks like a prayer rug and, in some ways, that is precisely how it functions. When a creative problem refuses to yield to ordinary methods, Elizabeth thinks on it while she sits on the worn but beautiful rug and cleans and oils her tack. Moving the supple leather through her fingers, cleaning and polishing the brass fittings, she often "happens" on the precise inspiration needed to finish the tricky portrait.

"I'm a Virgo," she laughs, "so maybe I believe in a particularly neat God, but I do find when I put physical things in order, spiritual questions also fall into place. There's something about my mucking out a stall that seems to inspire the creative angels to talk to me."

EXERCISE:

When our spiritual house is in order, great things come to pass for ourselves and others. Often when we are stymied in the outer world, it is time to turn a housekeeping hand to our inner world. All of us die, and we hope to have our affairs in order when we do. But few of us choose our moment of death. We can, however, choose to put our affairs in order.

List five areas of your life that could be brought to better health. Choose one from the list and put it in order.

1. Mend my relationship with my brother.
2. Revise my will to more accurately reflect my affections and intentions.
3. Visit with my cousins more regularly.
4. Write my parents weekly.
5. Write down the family recipes.

Spiritual housekeeping is sometimes called "karma cleanup."

FAMILY

I am not sure where we got the idea that trying to help people, our children especially, was a sign of having a dysfunctional personality with hideous tendencies toward codependency and control. When did it get modish and acceptable for the right reply to a mentioned parental concern become "Mmm . . . but it's not your job to help anymore, is it?"

When did we get the idea that kids were like cookies, "done" at eighteen or maybe twenty-one? When did we get the idea that help after that was just meddling? Meeting some neurotic need? I think I am rounding up the usual suspects here and wondering about the wisdom of a lot of therapy again. I suppose that it is true that some people are miserable because they worry too much about their children and do not have lives of their own. What I notice more often is people who are miserable because they aren't trying to actively help their kids, which is, after all, the way it has worked for centuries.

I believe in nepotism. I believe in helping hands. I believe in extended families, in family support, in sharing experience and battered-up old couches. I believe in home base and in tagging base and in family phone tag. I believe in "bring him by to dinner" and I believe in "let's build a family recipe file." I believe in "let's make a master list of what you think you'd like to do and see if we can help you do it."

Families are not perfect, but the basic plan had merit. Tinkering too much with the family as a basic concept is like going wholesale macrobiotic. You have to work pretty hard to get your basic nutritional needs covered and you may still end up anemic. In family life there is spiritual nutrition. Vitamins, minerals, and backbones. Yes, some parents can be too headstrong and smother their kids, but more parents are miserable and more kids are miserable from not interacting than have ever been miserable from sticking it out in the family stew. Where did we get the idea that family was optional? That it was a "birth unit" and not part of our life path? When did we start saying "I happened" to be born to this family?

If we look at our families with a little more open lens,

a lot more than "happened" is happening. Blue eyes, big noses, and musical gifts run in families. So does a sense of humor, a knack for piecrust, a first-rate tinkering ability, a love for dogs, a green thumb, an appetite for mysteries. Families used to be our favorite spectator sport. Families are what we used to do with Sundays. We watched family traits emerge—and even helped them emerge—before football. Sundays were getting the hang of poker, crossword puzzles, and bridge. They were checking out the progress on paneling the game room and admiring the two new quilt squares. Families suited up and showed up and they found continuity and humor as well as exasperation.

Families gave us context. We may differ from them and distinguish ourselves from them, but they give us a backdrop and they give us, most important, grounding. A little more work on connecting to our families and a little less on connecting to ourselves might actually serve to bring us the very spark of inner joy we are seeking.

E X E R C I S E :

This is a volatile, vulnerable, and valuable exercise. It will deepen your sense of self and self-respect. Do a little family archaelogy.

1. What interests do you share with your family? Send a token representing it to a relative.
2. Can you take a small action reaching out to a family member to share one of these interests? Do it.
3. Do you have a family picture gallery anywhere in your house? Make one.
4. Can you mark and observe family birthdays and special occasions on your yearly calendar? Do so.
5. Photograph the parts of your life your family does not see and send them a visual update.

BIRDS

～

My father loved birds. For ten of the last years of his life, he lived aboard a sailboat anchored in a Florida lagoon. From his deck, Dad and his Scottie dog, Blue, watched a steady parade of great blue herons, pelicans, seagulls, and the occasional snowy egret. When my father died, I kept a pair of his well-worn pajamas, his hearing aid, and a tiny pocket *Field Guide to North American Birds.*

My father himself was a birdlike man, frail and fierce. When his health went and he had to move back home from Florida, we found him a place in an old people's home and I bought him a bird feeder for outside his window. The birds never got a chance to come. My father hated being cooped up and managed, through an ad in the local newspaper, to find himself a small, sunny summer cabin on a wooded lagoon, loaded with birds. We worried about his living there. It was isolated and the long, winding drive to the cabin perilously bordered a new lagoon, but my father was adamant. He loved his birds and he would have them. Some of my happiest final visits involved sitting with Dad and Blue, watching silently to see what birds flashed through the foliage along his lagoon.

Yesterday, my sister Elizabeth called. She was excited. "I bought a martin house and put it way up on a tall pole," she reported. "It was such a Dad thing to do."

Joseph Campbell taught his students to "follow their bliss" if they wanted satisfying lives. My father followed his and it shaped his life. His love of birds continues to shape mine.

I first began keeping birds when I lived in Manhattan. I found that no matter how many times I got to Central Park, I still felt claustrophobic when I got home to my three rooms. "I miss birds," I thought one day when I was already missing my father. On impulse, I bought six baby birds and a gigantic cage.

"Mom, you bought six birds?" my daughter asked, her tone saying clearly "That's crazy."

"Yes. A flock," I answered, and I never regretted my indoor flock, although my lover and my houseguests felt differently, calling their mellifluous cacophony "racket."

My father particularly loved owls. My sister had a pair of them at her little red farm, and my father had more in his sheltering woods. He collected owl icons—etchings, small carved figures. We were always on the lookout for owls for Dad. They had to be "good owls, not the kitschy kind."

My father was a stubborn man. He refused to be sensible when he grew old. He refused to give up his freedom and he refused to give up his birds. We are so often taught that spirituality involves acceptance that we seldom realize that it equally involves nonacceptance. There are compromises we cannot and should not tolerate. My father would not compromise his independence—that and his love for birds.

High in the towering palm trees of my tiny neighborhood, I often spot a parti-colored flock of wild parrots. My father would have loved them.

As I write, seven enormous ravens wing to the top of a towering willow and a lone seagull cruises above them, looking down. Like my father, I have a small black dog and a collection of tiny owls.

BIRDS

When God got tired of using words
He expressed himself in birds.
Feathered, bright, and light of heart,
Birds were God's creative art.
Blue jay, hawk, and peregrine,
To be believed they must be seen.
Hummingbird, canary, finch,
God created every inch.

EXERCISE:

Allowing ourselves to love what we love is part of loving ourselves. We are each unique and irreplaceable. So, too, what we love is a reflection of our spiritual individuality. Pursuing an interest is a spiritual pilgrimage. Our loves lead us to a sense of wonder and grace. Over the door to the oracle of Delphi was printed two simple words: "Know thyself." Our true nature is often best revealed and developed by what we love.

Take pen in hand. Number from one to one hundred. List one hundred things you love. From that hundred, select the ten you love most. From that ten, select five. From that five, select one to begin with and follow that love with all your heart.

Take one concrete action to begin.

DIFFICULTY

⁓

I had gone to London to work and introduce some new books to the testy British press. English trips historically have been difficult for me, and this trip bore out the familiar pattern—hectic scheduling, scrambled appointments, mismatched agendas. It was with great relief that I found myself in the sitting room of a snug, deeply gardened house in St. John's Wood. I was there to visit a renowned clairvoyant, a gentle woman in her mid-sixties, with porcelain skin, lake-blue eyes, and a gracious, welcoming manner. Her spaniels curled cozily at her feet as she offered me tea, flicked on the tape recorder, and began her spiritual reading.

"First of all," she said, "what you're looking for sounds like the afterlife, not this one. You're craving peace, serenity, and ease. You'll get plenty of it then, but not now. That's not what this world is about." Despite myself, I had to laugh. The seer had accurately picked up my longing for tranquility.

"Ease is for the other side," she advised me, pausing to pet a spaniel. "We think that if we're in God's will, it's supposed to be easy. Sometimes God's will is difficult. We don't like it, but it's true."

Life is beautiful and difficult. That is its nature. None of us escapes pain, or loss, or loneliness. A spiritual life built on the notion that we can somehow evade or transcend the human condition is a spiritual life that is built on a lie. That lie tells us that difficult emotions and difficult times are nonspiritual and unacceptable. The lie tells us that if we find ourselves deep in the rapids of human experience, ricocheting with shock from the trauma of loss, we are doing something wrong.

The idea that if things are not going precisely as we would choose we are doing something wrong is one that most of us come to all too easily. It is tempting to think that if we just do something differently, the world will do as we wish. While we want to take responsibility for ourselves, taking responsibility for everything is grandiose.

There are times when we are doing nothing "wrong" and our lives are still difficult. The best of marriages endure arid times. The best of jobs may be by turns too stressful or too boring. All children worry their parents sometime. None of us has perfect health. The expectation

that if we are in good spiritual condition our lives will
be perfect is a false expectation. It may be more accurate
to say that our imperfect lives are perfect exactly as they
are.

EXERCISE:

In order to endure necessary difficulty, we must experience a sense of spiritual sustenance. We must use the
tools and attitudes that allow us to maintain a sense of
personal well-being even in an arduous passage. We
must:

1. Live one day at a time.
2. Put first things first.
3. Practice Easy Does It.
4. Let go and Let God.

If these expressions sound familiar, it is because they
are. They are the slogans that millions of people use to
endure the rigors of living with alcoholism. They are
also the American shorthand for universal spiritual
concepts.

Answer these questions on the page:

1. Are you living one day at a time? How do you err?
2. Are you putting first things first? What "things"?
3. Are you practicing easy does it? How could you?
4. Are you letting go and letting God? Try *not* doing one thing.

APOLOGIES

~~~

Although I yearn to home in New Mexico or the vertical canyons of New York, I currently live in a tiny, genteel, gentrified neighborhood—entirely filled with large, loud-barking dogs. The dogs are the deterrents to the rougher, wilder elements surrounding our neighborhood. Five blocks over they sell a lot of crack. Three blocks over we had drive-by shootings, but our street is safe—if you can bear the decibel level from all our dogs.

My contribution to the cacophony is two small dogs, one alto and one soprano. Last Sunday I let them out at eight A.M. and set up a ruckus.

"Julia!" I heard my neighbor's irritated voice. "Some of us are trying to sleep in!"

Chastised, I called the dogs back inside and made a note to myself to apologize later. Apology is a learned art for me.

"Which would you rather be? Right or comfortable?" my friend Julianna McCarthy once asked me.

Being "right" can be righteous and lonely. Julianna advised me to stop being "right" and start apologizing to mend relationships. I wanted to say "But! But! I *am* right. What about principles?" Then I decided to experiment instead.

"I'm sorry," I told the clerk whose arrogance had triggered me to be short-tempered. "I didn't mean to be so irritable."

The clerk, to my astonishment, softened her haughty attitude. "I just broke up with my boyfriend," she confessed.

"I'm sorry if I get impatient," I next tried out on the postal clerk.

"We are slow here," he laughed. "It's the land of mañana, don't you know that?"

"I'm sorry," I next tried out on my recent ex-husband. "Sometimes it takes me a while to hear your point of view."

"I know what you mean," he laughed. "I'm that way with you."

Apologies are not manipulative, but if they were, they'd be successful. Adversarial feelings seem to melt in the face of conciliatory softness. A mark is taken off when we apologize and often a second mark is taken off in return.

"I'm so sorry about my dogs," I told my neighbor. "I'm still used to living on a ranch where a barking dog at five

A.M. is normal. Forgive me." (I didn't say, "P.S. I'm moving back to New Mexico as soon as I can.")

"You forgive *me*," my neighbor countered. "I was so crabby."

After that exchange, we both grinned ruefully.

Without my apology I would never have learned my neighbor's progress on her novel. I would not have learned the name of her best and most fragrant rose. Worse yet, stuck in my righteousness—"City people. They sleep in forever"—I'd have missed the chance to forge a friendship.

"An apology doesn't mean you were awful," explains my friend Julianna. "It means you were human."

To my vast surprise, I find I rather like being human— even more than I like being "right."

EXPERIMENT:

Apologies are the art of spiritual housekeeping. They help to put and keep our lives in order. And yet an apology is not so simple as "I'm sorry." It involves the future as well as the past. "I'm sorry for what I did, *and* I'll never do it again." Where appropriate, it also involves the present: "Here is how I intend to make it up to you."

Sometimes, the best preparation for spiritual

housecleaning is a bit of physical housecleaning. Choose a messy area of your life, an area where you have delayed rehabilitation. It may be your overflowing desk, your dirty kitchen cabinets, your untidy tool area, your dirty car. Pick *something* that you can put in order. Do exactly that while contemplating the spiritual one. It works like this:

"I'm going to scrub and paper the shelves of the kitchen cabinets. Then I'm going to call Jane and tell her how much I miss our friendship and how sorry I am that I gossiped about her." The self-worth that comes from the physical action helps us to execute the spiritual action.

Now, execute it.

EASE

It is a chill and misty twilight with an ocean haze blurring the streetlamps. Seasons are subtle in Southern California, but they do exist. Winter is coming on and gardens are taking on winter drab. Tonight the mist erases the tops of the palm trees so they look like broomsticks, not feather dusters. All of this strikes me as sinister because I am worrying about my friend Stephen. He's into what you might call the Bud Lite Version of Spiritual S&M.

Stephen and I have been friends for twenty years, since he was a struggling New York actor and I was a young playwright eking out a living writing for magazines, living on Thai noodles and espresso. Over the years, I've watched Stephen's considerable talents repeatedly subverted by his spiritual conviction that if something was unbearably difficult and punitive, it must somehow be good for him and his art.

Like many of us, Stephen believes in spiritual hardship but not spiritual ease. He listened to Joseph Campbell say "Follow your bliss" and allowed himself to open the door to a life in the arts. Once there, however, he forgot about bliss or ease as a guiding principle. His self-denying Calvinism reared its head disguised as "spiritual growth."

The things that came to Stephen easily—film work, commercials, radio voice-overs—he considered to be unimportant. He not only looked gift horses in the mouth, he swatted them on the rump and chased them out the door. Time and again he drifted away from opportunity and toward adversity. This exquisitely rationalized self-sabotage was always presented to his friends—and to himself—as an opportunity for spiritual growth.

First, there was the wildly dysfunctional theater company. A classically handsome leading man, he suffered through season after season in ill-fitting character roles. Next there was the impossible marriage to the beautiful leading lady who was as selfish and greedy as a Disney villainess.

Calling it spiritual searching, Stephen has grown progressively more depressed. "I keep thinking I should be able to handle this," he tells me. "I keep thinking there's a lesson in here."

Sometimes, the spiritual lesson we are meant to learn is "This is unacceptable." Battered wives learn that lesson when they finally walk out, when they stop saying God wants them to stay with a battering husband because "marriage is sacred"—as if they themselves are not.

Whenever we believe in a punitive God bent on doling out lessons, we lock ourselves into a parent-child relationship with our spirituality. We accept the unacceptable, trying to be like good boys and girls with an arbitrary and authoritarian teacher. Whenever we place an institution ahead of human dignity we are believing in a conservative and hierarchical God. Stephen believed in acting as an institution and in so doing damaged himself as an actor. He believed in marriage as an institution and damaged himself as a husband. No career, no marriage, no affiliation with an outer form deserves precedence over our inner worth.

The thickening mist has just darkened into night. A phone call from Stephen reveals he's just been offered a pair of teaching jobs that would bring him financial freedom and an enjoyable creative outlet. What a nightmare for him!

"I'm thinking about them," he tells me. So accustomed is Stephen to misery that opportunity looks foreign and threatening. Turning over the offers, he keeps looking for the lead lining.

"I think I'd actually enjoy teaching," he says, clearly baffled by the prospect.

I am hoping that the mist will burn off in the night and that Stephen will have the clarity to accept "ease" as a spiritual possibility.

EXERCISE:

At the root of our anxious overexertion lies the deep-seated fear that we will not be taken care of, that we will be abandoned or betrayed by others, by ourselves, and by God. The most effective antidote to this haunting fear is the practice of gratitude, enumerating ways we have been cared for. This conscious and concrete enumeration of people, events, things, and conditions for which we feel grateful eases the heart.

Select a piece of "safety music"—music that cradles your heart and creates a sense of safety. Light a stick of incense, find a comfortable pillow. Lie flat on your back and audibly—yes, out loud—count your blessings.

CONTINUITY

Ours is a "cup of soup" society with microwave meals and hurry-up lifestyles that send us rushing forward without spiritual nurturance. The home-cooked meal has been replaced by McDonald's, whose golden arches can seem like an old friend.

A sense of continuity can go a long way toward giving us a sense of safety and spiritual connection. Seeing someone who knew and cherished you when you were young can make you feel seen and cherished when you are older. When we lived in small towns and our lives were less fragmented and frantic, we often had these spiritual markers in people as diverse as the postman, the butcher, the mechanic, and the hairdresser or barber. We grew up alongside people whom we knew and who knew us. They knew our parents and our siblings and we knew theirs. We witnessed each other's lives and, in doing that, we honored them. This created a sense of continuity and perspective. Hard times were then hard times and not a summing up of all we had done or chosen.

Continuity used to be a gift of life. Now it is an elected gift that we can choose to give to ourselves and to others. The Christmas card, the postcard, the photos sent back from our new home on the other coast—each of these small gestures creates a track of love to travel on. Sometimes to feel continuity, we must express it ourselves. We must take the time to write the postcard to an elderly aunt. We must take the time to mail off the box of toffee to the retired teacher who straightened out your grammar and your life.

In 12-Step programs, members are encouraged to find "a home group." That group serves to anchor the continuity of its members. The Sunday night candlelight meeting stands in many modern lives for the potluck at Aunt Fran's. Members return weekly and report in on the spills and chills of living, the new job or marriage undertaken, the growing pains at mid-stride in a career, the worry over a child's drug use or troubled relationship—all of these are shared and noted in the picture album of continuity that a home group provides. A church affiliation may serve the same function. So can Thursday night bridge—and "bridge" is the operative word for most of us.

We need to bridge our sense of loneliness and disconnection with a sense of community and continuity even if we must manufacture it from our time on the Web and our use of calling cards to connect long distance. We must "log on" somewhere, and if it is only in cyberspace, that is still far better than nowhere at all.

E X E R C I S E :

This exercise may create sorrow, but it will yield joy. Answer in writing.

1. In what ways do you build continuity into your life? List them.
2. In what further ways could you build continuity into your life? Try one.
3. What friends do you now "log on" with? Do so.
4. Who else could you "log on" with? Try this.
5. Do you formally "log on" with God at least once a day? Have you considered sending e-mail?

Alright, try a God letter.

DISAPPOINTMENT

Tragedy we can deal with. We weather the staggering blow. Our friends rally. We drop to our knees. We weep. We survive. What we cannot deal with, not well, is the steady drip, drip, drip of disappointment. With any luck, tragedy makes us strong and compassionate. Unless we are vigilant, disappointment makes us bitter.

When tragedy strikes, we may find we have the rudiments of wisdom. "This is big," we tell ourselves, as do our friends. We know enough not to expect ourselves to function like automatons. We muster a little self-love, grateful we can function at all "under the circumstances." Tragedy, terrible as it is, can be a spiritual tonic. Its stepsister, disappointment, can be a spiritual toxin.

Like the kind of environmental poisoning that comes from chemicals or radiation, the toll taken by repeated disappointment may be almost too subtle to notice. There is a gradual, and subtle, leaching of optimism. Enthusiasm and vitality diminish, all seemingly without cause. "For no reason" depression takes hold and we find ourselves emotionally shut down, devoid of inspiration or the impetus to find it. "What happened?" we may eventually rally enough to ask.

"Nothing happened," we answer, meaning "Nothing big." Disappointment by definition is small, something "that shouldn't bother us" and so we discount our disappointments, we diminish our disappointments, and we judge ourselves for feeling them at all.

Disappointment brings out self-loathing in most of us. We feel we should be above, or beyond, whatever it is we're feeling.

"Lighten up. It's no big deal," we tell ourselves when we feel the tears start welling up.

"Goddammit. Grow up," we snap at ourselves when a canceled dinner date plummets us into the depths.

When tragedy strikes, we know enough to share it, but when disappointment rears its head, we muzzle ourselves and try to tough it out. Yanking in our emotional bootstraps, we demand that we "get over it," whatever it is. Stoicism is demanded. Compassion for ourselves is out of the question.

"What are you sniveling about?" we snap at ourselves, perfect stand-ins for Cinderella's wicked stepsisters. Self-contempt, self-loathing, and self-condemnation rear their heads. We are disappointed in ourselves for being disappointed. Our situation lacks compelling grandeur, and so do we.

Nonsense. Disappointment is endemic to the human condition. We must accept that and ourselves. A little tenderness is called for, manufactured if need be.

I believe in weeping over disappointments. I call it "watering the heart" so the garden of life can continue to take root there and grow.

EXERCISE:

It is our unmourned losses that become the scar tissue of the heart. We carry an unnamed and unrecognized burden in the form of losses we have experienced but not properly mourned. Set aside an hour of quiet time. Divide a sheet of paper into three vertical columns. In column one, list your unmourned losses. In column two, list a healing action you could take regarding that loss. In column three, list a friend, sponsor, therapist, or minister with whom you can share the details of your disappointment. Set a gentle schedule with yourself for clearing your loss list.

Whenever we are experiencing an arduous pas-

sage, a spot-check inventory of our use of these concepts can help us to weather better the hard times.

1. Are you living with your difficulty a day at a time
   or are you projecting a future of misery? Do you
   find a way to balance some enjoyment in every
   day?
2. Are you practicing first things first, giving yourself
   the necessary self-care of good food, good rest,
   and moderate exercise? Do you reach for support
   as needed?
3. Are you setting realistic goals for yourself? Are
   you succumbing to a heightened sense of drama,
   deriving your self-worth from a misplaced martyrdom?
4. Are you remembering to ask for spiritual support?
   Do you allow yourself encouragement of prayer
   or spiritual reading? Are you forgetting that there
   is a God and acting like one yourself? Are you remembering that not only you, but those you love,
   have a God of their own?
5. What can you do today to nurture and enjoy
   yourself?

Compassion does not mean feeling sorry for ourselves or others. Compassion means feeling empathy
for ourselves and others. It means asking "Where does

it hurt?" and listening to the answer. Then it means responding appropriately. In other words, action may not mean the soothing words "There, there." It might mean the challenging words "Try this." Most spiritual traditions contain some forum for complaint. Make the page that forum now.

One more time, make three vertical columns. In column one, list what hurts. In column two, list *why* it hurts. In column three, list what you can do about it. Your pains may be regrets, resentments, or actual physical aches. Whatever their form, there is ordinarily a compassionate action, however small, available to you. Make your action concrete and specific to the particular pain involved. If you regret your lack of education, don't take a hot bath, sign up for a course. If you feel bad about your relationship with your sister, tackle mending it. What you are after here is sweet specificity.

DROP THE ROCK

A lot of the time, when we decide to work on our spirituality, we treat God like we are partners trying to save a bad marriage. You know the drill: We get very serious, very determined to "work this thing out." What happens then? We get so busy working on our relationship to God that we stop having it. We go into self-help mode and start reading a lot of books on our dysfunctional God relationship. We seek out expert advice. We do not do what actually works when a relationship is in trouble. We do not circle back to "Let's drop the rock and play a little, let's go to the movies."

God might love to go to the movies with us or for a walk on the beach or out for a malted. God might like to just spend time or go for a bike ride or hear our unedited thoughts instead of our carefully prepared statements, our formal, spiritually correct prayers. In other words, God might be like the guy who actually likes you and wants a relationship, not like the guy who just wants a blonde on his arm and a trophy relationship. God might be real and might be interested in our being real right back.

Anytime an intimate relationship goes south, it's because it doesn't feel safe to be real. It's because we've begun to edit, to get stuck in roles, to feel pinched off, pinched up, and serious. We start getting angry and say "This is what I think and this is what I need" instead of "Jesus, honey, I'm pretty miserable and I need either Häagen-Dazs or sex or a good cry or to go to the movies or I don't know what— aargh!"

God could probably do with a few more "I don't know what—aargh!" prayers. God could probably do with a few more "Let's just hang out" dates, a few more times of "Let's take the dog to the dog park and laugh at the puppies." Like any other partner, God probably would like it if we lightened up and liked a few things once in a while. Maybe God needs football on Sundays more than our resentful presence at church. "Let's go for a drive, God" might be a better idea than hitting God up with the St. Francis prayer. God may want to help us be an instrument of humor rather than of peace.

Agendas get in the way of relationships. They introduce a note of goose-step where chums-chums might be preferable. We talk about the "love of God," but we don't ever think much about wooing God. A good long-term relationship usually begins with a few laughs and spending time together. An occasional bunch of flowers is a good idea. Foot rubs are terrific, and if the laughs can hang around, usually so can the partners.

We don't talk very much about the laughing side of God. We act as if God is serious and important and pissed off and we had better toe the line. We don't look at the physical world and deduce, as we might, that God loves to doodle and experiment and actually likes peppy and willful things like puppies and maybe us. We so often fall into being exhaustively grown-up with God, a partner in a rotten marriage, we get this "It's not me, I'm perfect" thing going.

"I pray? Don't I? I meditate!" ("I do your goddamn laundry, don't I, God?")

As in most relationships, a little less work and a little more listening might work fine. It just might "play."

Drop the Rock

I wanted to be closer to my God,
"I'll give up everything, you don't need to prod."
I gave up sex and drinking and smoking,
I also gave up all my joking.
And God began to disappear
Saying, "You're not fun, I'm out of here."

EXERCISE:

Use your pen to puncture your martyrdom.

1. Are you convinced that misery is spiritual? Who taught you this? Write about it.
2. Do you believe difficulty earns you brownie points in heaven? List five punitive situations you have endured out of a sense of spiritual "should."
3. Do you feel morally superior when you're suffering? Write a dialogue between your martyr and yourself. Use Q & A to get your martyr to talk.
4. Do you believe in a solemn God? List five happier ones.
5. Are all of your "spiritual lessons" depressing?

Then, bake yourself cookies.

VISIONS

⌒

You could say they're a lot like daydreams, just more convincing. "Compelling" might be the right word. I'm talking about the spiritual experiences that some people call visions and the psychiatrically inclined call delusions.

I had a particularly strong series of these experiences six years ago. They began in England, first as an audio track, and then with visuals. They covered a wide range of metaphysical topics, centering chiefly on our largely unused and unsuspected creative powers. When I got back home to New Mexico, the experiences continued, changing their focus from the personal to the planetary. I felt like I was in an Imax film, *The March of Time*. Faces of the ancestors, an overview of earth, a harrowing review of human suffering in many forms preceded an overwhelming sense of compassion and equality. I sat on the grass under the apple tree to the east of my adobe house and watched spiritual events unspool in my consciousness like a long SenSurround documentary on what I was intended to know and how I was intended to live. As I sat under the apple tree day after day, some of my friends became interested, some intrigued, and some alarmed. Depending upon their perspective, I was having a nervous breakdown, a shamanic experience, or a creative breakthrough. The consensus might have been all of the above.

Spiritual experiences happen to all of us and they happen all the time. They range from the subtle and playful to the dramatic, from the seemingly coincidental to the convincingly life-altering. Perhaps because they may lock you up when you do it, we don't talk very much about spiritual experiences. Their reality to us may remain our guilty secret. Sharing that reality can provoke the skeptically inclined to trot out their identified patient voice, as they certainly did of me.

"Now, now, Julia, what's the phrase you keep hearing? 'Body of sound, body of light, body of sound, body of light?' That's gibberish."

And when you respond, "No, actually, that's the foundation of the universe," they look at you with grave concern.

"Maybe you're schizophrenic. You're hearing voices? Maybe you're manic-depressive. Maybe you're . . ."

"Off your rocker" is what they're thinking. And there's

not much point in arguing. You may do better, as I did, to turn to literary sources. I read endlessly on shamanic experiences. Been there, done that, I concluded. I read on Kundalini experiences. Yes, yes, ditto there. I read the spiritual autobiographies of Hindus and Christian mystics. The more I read, the more it seemed to me that an awful lot of people, from an awful lot of traditions, had seen an awful lot of pretty much the same things. "All roads lead to home. I mean Om," I began joking. The visions had told me pretty much the same thing. Far from making me feel different and special, my experiences made me feel the same, ordinary, and interconnected. If I felt more spiritual, everyone also felt more spiritual to me as well. In the big picture, we were doing better than I might have thought. We were lurching in the right direction, and what were a few millennia between friends?

My musicals *Avalon* and *Magellan,* my creativity books and my prayer books, my plans and my poetry, at least a dozen pieces of work to date, have all seemed to bubble forward as a result of my spiritual slide show. Over the years I've encountered others who have had experiences—they sometimes use the word "awakenings"—like my own. I've gradually reached the conclusion that such spiritual experiences are more common than we acknowledge and may perhaps become more common still as we deepen our exploration of the spiritual practices that may invite them. I have shared this thumbnail sketch of my own experiences on the chance that others might reveal more of theirs. My theory is, if we can get our spiritual experiences out of the closets and into the streets, we might feel safer there.

EXERCISE:

The tabloids are full of weird spiritual experiences. So are our lives, if we are willing to see them.

1. Do you believe in visions or even "glimpses"? Write on this.
2. Do you know anyone who's had one? Write on this.
3. Have you yourself had a vision? Please collage this *and* write about it.
4. Did you tell anyone? Who could you safely tell?
5. Would you tell anyone? Tell someone. If that feels unsafe, write a dialogue scene where you imagine telling someone.

LOVE LETTERS

I think God's like everybody else. Phone calls are fine, but it's nice to get a letter once in a while. I write to God a lot. I sit down, scrawl out "Dear God and Higher Forces," and then I report in. Sometimes it feels like a field report, like I am writing home from the front: "We've got a prowler. I think maybe I should sell the house. The police can't catch him and I'm pretty terrified." Other times, it's a little less pitched. "I am really missing John and I am hoping you are taking good care of him. I don't have anybody to talk to about my dreams right now and it's making me sad. Could you look around for a friend for me?"

Sometimes my letters are a little entitled: "You know what would make me really happy? Hint-hint." Other times they are flora and fauna reports: "The neighbor on my left has a rose the size of a saucer with crimson edging on it that's pretty fancy." (In case God hadn't noticed.)

When I'm in a funk or a snit, I can resist writing God. I can go radio silent and figure "God knows anyway." Actually, I am sulking and I do a lot better when I take pen to page and gripe. "Dear God, Is this hellish mess for my spiritual advancement? I am finding it pretty ungroovy and I am out of ideas about it, so send some, would you?"

I do a lot of "send some" prayers, which I have been told are the lowly prayer form "Gimme-gimme," but I know with my own daughter, I like giving her things and if she is muddling along without something and not asking, I sometimes get mad. "Why didn't you tell me what you needed? That's easy!" I have a hunch that God gets a kick out of helping just like I do.

My concept of God isn't really Santa Claus, although I have had lots of experiences of God that could promote that notion. I tend to find wonderful and imaginative places to live and that, I think, may be the Mrs. Claus aspect of God. I sit down and write "I need two work spaces and light and a reasonable rent and I wish I could see a church steeple like I did from that great old apartment I had on North Ninth Avenue. . . ." I usually get the full shopping list with extras. And not, I don't think, because I am God's favorite, but because I have asked.

My experience of God is of a benevolent, listening, interactive Something, and when I communicate with It, I feel better. For all I know, the letters may pile up unopened, but writing them is good for me—and it certainly feels like they get read.

I have gone through stages where I have wanted a much more intellectually acceptable way to relate to God. I have been embarrassed when people were into elaborate and formal routines and I was dropping postcards and thank-you notes. And yet, there was something wonderful about having a written trail.

"I wish . . ." I would write, and scribble off maybe twenty wishes ranging from "I had a decent haircut" to "I had an idea for a new musical." Almost behind my back, and with sometimes insulting speed (and sometimes not), the wishes would begin to get mysteriously ticked off.

I keep a large blue and white dragon-entwined God Jar for what I think of as the Special Delivery letters. The jar is stuffed with "Problems I can't solve" and "People I want You to look after" and "Ideas that won't rise properly" and "Here's a photo, now do you know who I mean?"

Sometimes, I think God is an electrical current that moves into the world through my hand when I write. A sort of spiritual form of magic ink like when an animator scribbles out a sketch of Mickey and the next thing you know he is racing around the desk. I do know that something magical happens when I write to God. It's like "I write" and God "rights" things.

E X E R C I S E :

If God wrote the Bible, the least you can do is answer a few more simple questions. Back to the page.

1. Have you learned to pray on the page?
2. Have you ever written God a funny valentine?
3. Have you ever sent God a thank-you note?
4. Do you write God an angry letter to clear the air when you are miffed?
5. How about a love letter?

Choose one of the above and write it. Execute the others later.

ROOTS AND WINGS

Hatha yoga or t'ai chi
We each dance the dance we've found
Mudras are to the body
What pitch is to the sound.
Pick the dance you like the best,
That suits you to the ground
Gestures are the structure
Our key is built around.

We are all like tuning forks
With a truth we're bringing in.
The toning is the tuning
Of the frequencies we've been!
This is what the Sufis taught
When they learned how to spin.
This is why the ragas
Modulate the day we're in.

Architecture is to music
What a building is to boards
What a blueprint is to building
The ratio is to chords.
We're not made of stone or granite
But this is what I'll say

Proportion relates to planets
Exactly the same way.

The ratio sets our radio
And determines the wave we play.
Astrology to personality
Is our spiritual DNA!
Numerology like astrology
Is another numbers game.
They're all mother tongue to someone
What they're speaking is the same.

We've elected and selected
The chord we're playing out,
Holding to our frequency
Is what the game's about!
Listening takes practice
So does voicing what we've heard—
This is why they tell us:
The beginning was the word.

All roads lead us back to Rome
And, further on, back home
We are all remembering chords and codes
Stuck in our bones.
The toning whale, pentatonic scale,

The vowels "a" and "e"
They are all a part of sound's vocabulary.

The Kabalah, the Mandala,
Treble clef, the Tree of Life—
They are all expressing
The eternal archetype.
We—each of us—are traveling
Our own way back home,
We are all unraveling
The mystery of "om."

Botanists, biologists,
Guerrillas in the mist!
All of us are searching
For the puzzle piece we missed.
Anthropologists, psychologists,
Physicists and fools,
All of us are looking
For a working set of rules.

Herbalists, like gerbils, must
Dig deep to find their truth.
The etymologists of ecologists,
They go back to the root.
But their scary roots and berries
All seem to bear some fruit,

All of us have treasure maps—
They just show different routes!

Call it preference or systemology,
We all choose the one that suits.
Call it fate or reflexology,
We find our hiking boots.
Call it karma, call it dharma,
Call it fate or simply path,
We are all of us traveling
On our own way back.

Use Tantra or a mantra,
Use a whistle or a drum
All of us are turning to
The same eternal hum.
As I said back at the beginning,
The listening heart is home.
If you take that word apart,
You'll find it's built on "om."

ABOUT THE AUTHOR

Julia Cameron is the author of seventeen books, fiction and nonfiction, many plays and movies. She happily lives again in the high desert of New Mexico where she busies herself with musicals, movies, poetry, horses, and dogs. She also lives half the time in New York City, where her theatre work is often staged. No longer a public teacher, she taught extensively for two decades in venues ranging from London to Los Angeles, from Esalen to *The New York Times.* Her work on creativity features the bestselling books *The Artist's Way, The Vein of Gold,* and *The Right to Write.*